# Real, Raw, and Radiated

*My Emotional Journey with Breast Cancer*

**By Jessica Dickens**

# Copyright

Copyright © 2025 by Jessica Dickens

All rights reserved.

No part of this book may be reproduced, distributed, or transmitted in any form or by any means, including photocopying, recording, or other electronic or mechanical methods, without the prior written permission of the author, except in the case of brief quotations embodied in reviews and certain other noncommercial uses permitted by copyright law.

ISBN: 979-8-218-78677-9

Printed in the United States

This is a work of nonfiction. This is not medical, legal, or financial advice. This content is for informational purposes only and is not professional advice.

# **Dedication**

To my husband, my daughter, and my mom—

There are no words big enough to express my gratitude for the way you carried me through this journey. You took on the weight of my struggles without hesitation, making my hardest days easier in ways I never could have expected. Your love, care, and unwavering support were my foundation when everything else felt unsteady.

To my husband—your strength and devotion never wavered. You stood beside me through every fear, every tear, and every difficult moment, showing me the true meaning of "in sickness and in health."

To my daughter—you gave so much of yourself, stepping into a caretaker role with so much love and patience. Your quiet strength and constant presence made sure I never felt alone. Your compassion and kindness truly helped me heal.

To my mom—you were there in every way possible, reminding me that no matter how old I get, a mother's love is a force unlike any other.

And to everyone who showed me kindness—whether through a message, a meal, a gift, a hug, a small break from reality, or a simple moment of understanding—your support lifted me up and reminded me that I was never fighting alone.

This book is for all of you. Thank you from the depths of my heart.

# Table of Contents

**Copyright**

**Dedication**

**Introduction**

**Chapter 1** *From Routine to Revelation: The Mammogram That Changed Everything*

**Chapter 2** *Hope and Trepidation: The Long-Awaited Call*

**Chapter 3** *Embracing the Unknown: A Journey Through the Numbers and Stories*

**Chapter 4** *Timing Is Everything: Bad News on the Brink of Adventure*

**Chapter 5** *Unexpected Setbacks: When Plans Change*

**Chapter 6** *A Room Full of Answers: The Oncologist's Wisdom*

**Chapter 7** *Facing Fear: Unseen Trials*

**Chapter 8** *Strength in Vulnerability: The Power of Support*

**Chapter 9** *A Sanctuary of Sunshine: Home Is Where the Heart Is*

**Chapter 10** *Facing Fear (Again): The MRI Challenge Revisited*

**Chapter 11** *The Weight of Failed Attempts: The Struggle Continues*

**Chapter 12** *The Battle of the Third Attempt: Conquering the MRI*

**Chapter 13** *A Storm Within: The Weight of Unseen Wounds*

**Chapter 14** *Anchored by Support: Facing the Unknown Together*

**Chapter 15** *Fractured Normalcy: Living in Two Worlds*

**Chapter 16** *The Ticking Clock: Life Moves Forward, But So Does the Fear*

**Chapter 17** *A Circle of Strength: Wrapped in Love on Surgery Day*

**Chapter 18** *Right Place, Right Time: The Unexpected Blessing of Perfect Timing*

**Chapter 19** *The Support Network: Balancing Love and Burden*

**Chapter 20** *Silent Battles: The Loneliness Within Support*

**Chapter 21** *Behind the Smile: The Burden of Hidden Suffering*

**Chapter 22** *Beyond the Fear: Finding Strength in Answers*

**Chapter 23** *The Rising Tide: The Unrelenting Waves of Emotions*

**Chapter 24** *The Weight of Worry: Easing the Fear Through Answers*

**Chapter 25** *The Crimson Wing: Finding Strength in Unexpected Symbols*

**Chapter 26** *A Fortress of Love: Strength in Those Who Stand Beside Me*

**Chapter 27** *Moments of Clarity: Discovering My Inner Strength*

**Chapter 28** *A Moment of Relief: Farewell to Radiation, Forever Grateful*

**Chapter 29** *Lessons Carried Forward: A Moment to Reflect*

**Chapter 30** *A Fork in the Road: Choosing a Path Forward*

**Chapter 31** *Finding Refuge: Mountains, Water, and the Path to Peace*

**Chapter 32** *A Fragile Heart: Carrying the Unspoken Pain*

**Chapter 33** *Choosing Surgery: Protecting My Future*

**Chapter 34** *A Lesson in Grace: Learning to Heal, Inside and Out*

**Chapter 35** *The Voice Within: Trusting My Gut*

**Chapter 36** *Bones Tell a Story: Establishing a Baseline*

**Chapter 37** *Burning Through the Night: Sleep, Sweat, Repeat*

**Chapter 38** *Fear to Freedom: The Relief of Knowing*

**Chapter 39** *Silent Battles: Bravery, Love, and Letting Go*

**Chapter 40** *Standing Still: When Life Pauses but the World Moves On*

**Chapter 41** *A New Reflection: When the Mirror Shows Someone Stronger*

**The Technical Stuff and Diagnosis Breakdown**

**Resources I Found Helpful**

**About the Author**

# Introduction

I never imagined I would write a book about breast cancer. Then again, I never imagined I would hear the words, "You have breast cancer." But life has a way of surprising us, sometimes in the most challenging ways.

In May of 2024, my world got flipped upside down. I had built a life I loved—married to my high school sweetheart for 28 years, raising three incredible children who are now grown, and experiencing life in different places, from Japan to several states across the U.S. I thought I knew what challenges looked like, but nothing could have prepared me for the journey I was about to go through.

Breast cancer is often painted in broad strokes—either as a fight against an advanced and aggressive disease or as an easily treatable. But what about the in-between? What about the emotional rollercoaster, the uncertainty, the grief for the life you had before those words changed everything? I found myself searching for stories like mine—stories of women navigating a diagnosis that wasn't the worst-case scenario but was still life-altering. I wanted reassurance that my fears, my sadness, my overthinking, and my overwhelm were valid

This book is my story—honest, unfiltered, and deeply personal. It's about what it felt like to be diagnosed, the choices I faced, the emotions I wrestled with, and the lessons I learned along the way. My hope is that by sharing my journey, I can help others feel seen, understood, and less alone.

If you're reading this because you or someone you love is facing breast cancer, I want you to know that every experience is valid. No matter the stage, no matter the treatment plan, you are not alone in this.

This is my story. I hope it brings you comfort, strength, and the reminder that even in the hardest moments, we are in this together.

## Chapter 1

# From Routine to Revelation
## *The Mammogram That Changed Everything*

I've always been fairly diligent about preventative care—maybe not perfect, but I try. When I turned 40 in 2020, I knew it was time to start my annual mammograms. But life has a way of getting busy, and somehow, it wasn't until 2022 that I scheduled my first one. Better late than never, right? Life got busy, and I skipped my 2023 mammogram. But 2024 was going to be different—I vowed to prioritize my health. I had a plan: get my mammogram, take care of some dental issues, and schedule a full skin cancer screening. I was determined to check all the boxes, and the mammogram seemed like the perfect place to start.

On May 24, 2024, I finally went in for my routine-ish mammogram. The technician was friendly, chatting as she adjusted me into position. It's an oddly intimate experience—making small talk while a stranger handles your breast, positioning it just right. She mentioned she was new and that this facility still used an older machine, though she hoped they'd upgrade soon. After taking the images, she asked me to wait while she reviewed them. A couple of minutes later, she returned, saying she needed to retake one of the images of my left breast. *No big deal*, I thought. She was new, and I figured it was just part of the learning curve. I wasn't there because I had found a lump or had any concerns—this was purely preventative. So, I shrugged it off and was okay with her taking as many images as she needed.

A few days later, I received a call from the breast care center. They needed me to come back for a repeat mammogram—this time at a different location with newer, more advanced equipment. They also wanted to schedule an ultrasound, though it would only be necessary if the mammogram showed anything concerning. If everything looked clear, I could skip it.

I arrived for the repeat mammogram, feeling slightly less confident than I had the first time. I reassured myself that it was likely just a matter of getting clearer images and that I wouldn't need the ultrasound. The technician was professional and efficient, skipping the small talk and focusing on the task at hand. Mammograms are generally quick, and this one was even faster since they were only re-scanning my left breast. Within minutes, it was done.

I was instructed to wait while the radiologist reviewed the new images. They would return shortly to let me know if I was free to go—or if I needed the ultrasound. And, of course, the latter was exactly what happened. A few moments later, I was directed to the ultrasound room, my nerves tightening with each step.

The ultrasound tech was kind, her room a stark contrast to the sterile medical space where I had just had the repeat mammogram. A galaxy projector cast soft, shifting lights across the ceiling, accompanied by soothing music. It was clear this environment was designed to ease the anxiety of women like me, and in that moment, I was deeply grateful for it. As much as I love outer space and zen music, no amount of ambiance could change the fact that I was now staring at a screen, watching as a dark, round shape appeared—something that clearly didn't belong.

Still, I clung to the hope that it was nothing. I tried to stay rational—no family history, no lumps, nothing alarming. Maybe it was just a harmless fluid-filled cyst. I had a friend who had one drained recently—no big deal. But no matter how much I reassured myself, the unease settled in.

When the ultrasound was finished, the tech told me to wait while the radiologist reviewed my images and then she would come in and talk to me. I wished that I hadn't put my phone so far away, all I could do was lay there and watch the swirling galaxy lights, which ironically felt like my thoughts, deep, vast, and unknown. If I'd had my phone I would have texted my mom to distract my thoughts. Thankfully I didn't have to wait long, within minutes, the radiologist entered the room, her face serious. She explained that I had a solid mass in my left breast that needed further evaluation. An ultrasound-guided biopsy was recommended. My mind buzzed—solid mass. Not fluid-filled. Not a cyst. The words felt heavy, foreign.

Tears welled in my eyes. The doctor, sensing my growing panic, reassured me that nothing was confirmed yet. She urged me not to jump to conclusions. When she was done briefing me she said that I could take a few minutes to get dressed and process my thoughts but all I wanted was to get the hell out of that room. I quickly ditched the gown and put my shirt on, eager to escape to the solitude of my car, where I could call my husband and my mom—both of them could ground me in this surreal moment. A small part of me felt kind of bad to call with bad news.

As if the emotional weight wasn't enough, the timing was terrible. We were just days away from leaving for a long-awaited family vacation to Sandpoint, Idaho. How could this be happening now?

Later that day, I received another call—my biopsy was scheduled for the very next day. In a strange way, it was a relief. The waiting was already unbearable, and I was grateful I wouldn't have to endure it for long.

When I arrived for the biopsy, the nurse greeted me warmly, offering a heated blanket to ease my anxiety. I accepted it gratefully, appreciating the small comfort. The radiologist came in, explaining the procedure step by step. I dreaded the numbing injection, especially after too many unpleasant experiences at the dentist. But she reassured me— this was different. *"Dentists numb nerves, which is why it hurts so much. Here, we are numbing a small area of tissue, and the discomfort will be minimal"*. She was right. Just a quick pinch—nothing like what I had braced myself for.

The procedure itself was painless and quick. They gave me the option to watch on the ultrasound machine, I chose not to watch and she kindly turned the monitor out of my view. I felt like if I watched I might panic or at the least get a wave of anxiety. Instead I focused on the sensations. No pain, just the odd awareness that something was happening. The radiologist guided the needle with precision, taking three samples. She warned me that I would hear a loud popping sound with each extraction, I tensed—but it wasn't as bad as I expected. Just a sharp snapping sound, like a rubber band. I didn't feel any pain, just the pressure.

Once the samples were collected, she inserted a tiny titanium clip next to the mass—a marker for future mammograms to indicate that area had once been an area of concern. She explained that the samples would go to pathology, with one being sent for additional third-party testing. Results would take a few days, maybe longer for the external test. The breast care center nurse cautioned me that all results would be available in the MyChart app as soon as they came in, urging me not to Google anything I read. She admitted that she often struggles to follow her own advice, so if I did end up searching online like most people do, I should jot down my questions for her to address when she called. She assured me that she would personally reach out to review the results as quickly as possible.

Before I left, she gave me aftercare instructions and a small care package—a thoughtful gesture that caught me off guard. Inside was lotion, chapstick, chocolates, and a heart-shaped ice pack to ease swelling. *"Chocolate always helps with healing,"* she said with a smile. I wanted to cry, taking steadying breaths to keep my tears in check at least until I could get into my car. I was appreciative that she was so kind. Healthcare really needs more people like her.

Then, one final step—a mammogram to capture an updated image with the clip in place. Quick and painless.

And just like that, I was on my way.

Now, all I could do was wait.

## Chapter 2

# Hope and Trepidation
## *The Long-Awaited Call*

They had estimated the results would take three to four business days, but they appeared in the MyChart app just one day later. It's strange how, in just two weeks, I had gone from a routine mammogram to feeling paralyzed at the thought of reading my own results.

Here we go… Big words. Unfamiliar terms. No wonder the breast care center nurse had warned me that it might feel like a foreign language.

Carcinoma?

Wait—*what? As in cancer carcinoma?!*

Oh no.

I hesitated, hoping there was another meaning. Maybe carcinoma wasn't always cancer? I turned to Google. *"Are there non-cancerous carcinomas?"* Google's answer: *No.*

That's not good at all.

My thoughts spiraled, looping in frantic circles. *No family history. No lump. This doesn't make sense.* I tried to pull myself away from the screen. *No more Googling. No more MyChart.* The breast care center nurse had warned me about this exact moment but knowing that didn't make it any easier.

Then, the tears came—hot, relentless, unstoppable. Maybe it was fear. Maybe it was shock. Maybe it was both.

I stared at the pathology report, the words blurring through my tears. This can't be real.

And then, anger—sharp and unforgiving. At myself for skipping my mammogram last year. At the naive belief that waiting wouldn't matter. *What if I had had the mammogram last year?* The thought lodged itself deep in my chest, a weight I couldn't shake.

Ten minutes later, I was back in MyChart.

*Ductal carcinoma in situ (DCIS). Estrogen receptor strong positive. Invasive carcinoma.*

I couldn't stop myself—I typed, *What is...*

The words on the screen hit me like a ton of bricks. My breath caught in my throat. And now, I had to find the strength to tell the people I loved most—my husband, my kids, my family. The thought of saying those words out loud filled me with dread. My heart ached for them before I had even spoken a word.

Then, out of nowhere, an overwhelming wave of guilt and shame crashed over me. How could this be happening? Was I somehow responsible? I knew, logically, that wasn't true, but logic didn't stand a chance against the storm inside me.

I broke.

I wasn't just crying—I was sobbing, heaving, my entire body convulsing under the weight of my emotions. Grief, fear, disbelief—it all poured out at once. My husband held me as I unraveled, his arms wrapped around me, grounding me as best he could. But I couldn't speak. I couldn't stop. I could barely breathe.

Even after the sobs subsided, I felt like I was drowning. How do I have this conversation? How do I say, *"I have breast cancer"?* I kept imagining what it would feel like if my husband told me he had cancer. Or my kids. Or my parents. My heart would completely shatter.

Which is harder—telling the news or hearing it? I hope I never have to know the answer to that question.

How is this real? I don't have a family history. I don't feel a lump. Were there warning signs I missed? I opened my most recent blood work results—my white blood cell count was slightly elevated, but not enough to raise any red flags. Shouldn't I have more symptoms? Rapid weight loss? Fatigue? Pain?

Instead, all I felt was…disgusted. Embarrassed. Ashamed.

And then, guilty for feeling those things at all.

I couldn't even make sense of my own emotions. But maybe I didn't have to—not yet. For now, I just had to keep breathing.

CHAPTER 3

# Embracing the Unknown
## *A Journey Through the Numbers and Stories*

From the moment I heard the diagnosis, I became consumed by research. I've always been someone who craves data, statistics, and insight, but now, it wasn't just curiosity—it was survival. Breast cancer had suddenly become my reality, and I turned to the only source that might offer some answers to my growing uncertainty: *the internet.*

I devoured Google searches, scoured medical blogs, and combed through support groups, searching for someone—anyone—who had walked this exact path before me. I wasn't necessarily looking for stories of miraculous recoveries or unwavering bravery, though those were comforting. What I truly needed were facts. I needed to understand what would come next. What happens first? What do these test results mean? How do I prepare for the unknown?

All of this Googling happened before I even had my first conversation with the oncologist or the breast care center nurse. The thought of discussing my diagnosis with a cancer specialist felt bizarre, as though I had stepped into a version of my life that I didn't recognize. In complete disbelief that I was even in need of an oncologist.

As I sat in front of my computer, pathology report pulled up on my phone, I found myself frantically searching for definitions of unfamiliar terms. The numbers and statistics I uncovered were staggering. One in eight women in the United States will be diagnosed with breast cancer in their lifetime. Approximately 70-80% of breast cancers are estrogen receptor (ER) and progesterone receptor (PR) positive. But the statistic that hit me the hardest? Around 80-85% of breast cancer cases are *not* genetic.

How had I gone my entire life assuming that breast cancer was primarily hereditary? This realization felt like a punch to the gut. It meant that cancer didn't care about my lack of family history, it could still happen—was happening—to me.

Amidst the shock and disbelief, a sobering realization cut through the chaos—*I am so glad I chose 2024 to prioritize my health.*

What if I had waited another year? What if I had kept putting it off, assuming I had more time? The thought sent a chill through me. My diagnosis was already life-changing, but another year would have made it so much worse.

When I came across the phrase estrogen positive, I wasn't just shocked—I was angry. Angry at my body. Angry at the universe. But mostly, angry at the medical professionals who had dismissed my concerns for so long.

Since 2011, I had been searching for answers to a cycle of debilitating premenstrual symptoms. The stiff neck, aching back and hips, and relentless migraines had become my monthly reality. Each time I voiced my concerns to a doctor, I was met with a dismissive, *"You're too young for hormone testing,"* and was handed a prescription for migraine medication or a muscle relaxer. I felt brushed off, unheard, and minimized.

Hindsight is a cruel thing. Looking back now, I wish I had pushed harder for answers. I wish I had sought out functional medicine, demanded hormone testing, or at the very least, trusted my instincts that something wasn't right. But at the time, I didn't know what I didn't know.

Now, sitting here with a breast cancer diagnosis, I found myself stuck in a relentless cycle of blame—blaming the doctors for not taking me seriously, blaming myself for not being more assertive, and then blaming the doctors all over again. The emotions churned within me: frustration, regret, and resentment tangled together in a toxic mix.

I stared at my screen, a single thought looping over and over in my mind: *I knew my hormones were out of balance.* And now, I was facing breast cancer.

The what-ifs haunted me. What if I had pushed for answers earlier? What if someone had listened? What if this could have been caught sooner? But in the end, there were no answers—only the reality in front of me and the journey ahead.

## Chapter 4

# Timing Is Everything
## *Bad News on the Brink of Adventure*

The wait for the nurse's call felt endless, even though it had only been two days since my biopsy. When the phone finally rang, I set my iPad to record. I needed to be able to listen back later and share it with my mom, to process it on my own terms. Looking back, I'm so grateful I did, because the moment she said the words *"breast cancer"*, my mind went blank.

The breast care center nurse emerged like a beacon of hope. Her calm and reassuring demeanor soothed my nerves as she outlined the next steps. She proactively provided an overview of the process, detailing who would be calling to schedule my appointments. Her promise to be my advocate, a steady support throughout every phase of this journey, was a much-needed comfort. She informed me that I would soon hear from the medical oncologist, radiation oncologist, and surgeon's office. There was a possibility of additional tests or an MRI, but she assured me that after meeting with the specialists, I would have a clearer understanding of each step in the process. Every diagnosis is different, she explained, and soon I would have the details I needed.

Despite the weight of our conversation, I managed to hold back tears. I wasn't entirely sure why—maybe it was her soothing presence or the lingering shock—but I remained composed. As the news settled in, my thoughts shifted. In just two days, we were supposed to leave for Idaho. Would I have to cancel? The thought of missing the trip filled me with disappointment, as if everything was spiraling out of control.

Instead of assuming the worst, I decided to just ask. A small part of me was scared to hear the answer. *"Can I still go on vacation?"* I asked hesitantly.

She responded with warmth, *"You go. You go have fun. Nothing is better than laughing and having a good time."*

Flooded with relief—not just for myself but for my family, too. We had been looking forward to this trip for months, and missing it felt unimaginable. She then added something that felt like a lifeline: *this particular type of cancer is slow growing.* That reassurance gave me room to breathe, to think, and, for the first time since seeing that terrifying "C" word, I felt a flicker of hope.

Family vacations have always been a remedy for my soul, a chance to recharge and be reminded of what truly matters. The road ahead was uncertain—likely long and daunting—but one last getaway with the people I love most before the whirlwind of appointments began was exactly what I needed. More than anything, I needed a hug from my mom. I needed to hold her and be held by her.

I feel incredibly blessed to have such a wonderful family. The drive to Idaho was uneventful, but after hours together in the car, we eventually found ourselves giggling over silly moments. I'd be lying if I said my mind wasn't occupied with thoughts of my diagnosis, though. I had faced loss, grief, and hardship before, but this felt fundamentally different. It was as if there was a ticking time bomb inside me, stealing my breath and weighing heavily on my heart. I was still struggling to grasp how this had become my reality. Why me? Why now? The "C" word—seriously? My emotions ran in cycles: anger, sadness, frustration, disappointment, hope, strength, determination, guilt—and then back through them all over again.

On our way to Sandpoint, we stopped in Spokane for lunch with everyone, then headed to a beautiful church that held special significance for my aunt. Thankfully, they had visited the church the day before because it was not open for visitors. We were hoping to check it out too so it was a bit of a bummer that we couldn't go inside, but across the street was something unexpected and special: a labyrinth. There was a sign at the entrance that read:

*"St. John's Labyrinth: Polly's Path. The labyrinth offers an invitation to go on a walk—a spiritual walk. This walk, like life, has twists and turns. It is an opportunity to wind your way*

*toward the center, casting off the burdens, the pressures, the distractions you carry, while opening your mind and heart. At the center is a place of illumination—a place you may want to linger a while. A place that may invite prayer, meditation, peace. As you leave the center, you follow the same winding path that guided you in. On the way out, you prepare to join in the healing of the world, empowered for what lies ahead."*

Since my family had already visited the church the day before and my husband and kids weren't interested in walking a squiggly path in the light rain, they stayed in the car while I walked the labyrinth with intention. With every step, I reminded myself that this journey was mine to walk, and although I knew it wouldn't be easy, I had the strength to face it. In the center, I paused, taking a few steadying breaths, letting go of some of the worries I had been carrying. It felt so peaceful, almost overwhelming in its calmness. I almost cried—had I not been aware of the others waiting for me, I might have. But instead, I felt a quiet sense of peace wash over me.

As expected, being with my parents, aunt, uncle, and cousin filled my heart with warmth. Their presence was comforting, a reminder of the love that anchored me even in uncertainty. We spoke only briefly about my diagnosis—there were still too many unknowns, too many unanswered questions hanging in the air.

Then, in a moment of almost surreal irony, my cousin walked out wearing a breast cancer awareness shirt. I knew it wasn't for me—he had it for someone else—but suddenly, it felt deeply personal. It caught me off guard, making me smile, though that smile carried the weight of everything I was facing. My mom, on the other hand, couldn't hold back her emotions. The second she saw it, she burst into tears. The look on his face was priceless a mix of confusion and concern, as if he were silently asking, *What did I do?*

That same day, I got a call from the medical oncology office, calling to schedule my first appointment. A flood of emotions crashed over me—relief that things were moving forward, fear of what was to come.

Later, we took a short drive up to Schweitzer Mountain, a brief escape from reality. We snapped a few family photos, capturing a moment that at the time felt like every other family vacation picture. But looking at it now, I see so much more. I see the people I love standing beside me. I see a version of myself on the brink of something life-altering, holding onto hope even as fear lingered beneath the surface. It wasn't just a beautiful photo—it was the beginning of a new chapter; one I never saw coming.

This was just the beginning.

## Chapter 5

# Unexpected Setbacks
## *When Plans Change*

On the final day of our family vacation, we were blindsided—not just one, but two people in the house tested positive for COVID. Then two quickly became three. Disbelief quickly turned to action as my husband, ever the protector, sprang into cleaning mode, sanitizing every surface in sight to minimize my risk of exposure. I could see the worry in his eyes, and he wasn't the only one concerned. Everyone tiptoed around me as if I were made of glass, but strangely, I wasn't as afraid as they were. Maybe it was because, despite my recent diagnosis, I didn't feel sick. It made me wonder—how compromised was my immune system, really? Still, we took every precaution. Everyone took a COVID test. Those who tested positive were quarantined in their rooms, and the rest of us kept our distance. But even with all the caution, there was no way I was leaving without hugging my parents. Not being able to hug the others, though, broke my heart.

The drive home was even more exhausting than the drive there. Fatigue, paranoia, and an eerie silence settled over us. We stopped along the way to pick up some COVID tests—just in case. And it was a good thing we did, because the very next day, my daughter and I started feeling sick. We tested, and there it was—positive. Somehow, my husband and son managed to avoid it, but my daughter and I weren't as lucky. The virus hit us fast and hard, forcing us to quarantine in my bedroom for several days. Out of the nine of us on the trip, seven ended up getting it.

Even through the fever and exhaustion, one thought refused to let go—my oncology appointment was in two days. But there was no way I could walk into that office while battling COVID. I could have forced myself to go, pushed through the misery, but the risk of exposing another cancer patient was unthinkable. I couldn't do that to someone else.

So, with a heavy heart, I made the dreaded call to reschedule.

*"We'll have to push it back ten days,"* the receptionist said.

A wave of panic crashed over me. Ten more days of waiting, of uncertainty, of feeling like this ticking time bomb inside me was gaining momentum. The emotional rollercoaster I had just started to get a grip on came hurtling back at full speed—anger, sadness, fear, frustration. The what-ifs spiraled in my mind. I had done everything I could to prepare for that appointment, and now, suddenly, I was stuck in limbo.

All I could do was wait for ten more days!

CHAPTER 6

# A Room Full of Answers
## *The Oncologist's Wisdom*

To say I was nervous about meeting with the oncologist would be an understatement. My emotions were all over the place—hope and dread battling for control. I had no idea what to expect. Thankfully, I didn't have to face it alone. My husband took time off work to be with me, and I was beyond grateful for his support.

As we sat in the waiting room, a sobering reality washed over me—I actually needed to be here. The oncology office required masks, which served as a stark reminder of the severity of my situation and that of the other patients around me. My eyes wandered to a small basket on the counter labeled "Free Mastectomy Seatbelt Pads," and my mind spun. Would I need one of those? Before I could dwell too long, I heard my name.

Everything felt surreal, like a slow-motion scene in a movie. My heartbeat pounded in my ears as my husband squeezed my hand, reassuring me that I was not alone. We walked together to the exam room, where I snapped a quick photo of us—my rock, my unwavering support. I sent it to my mom with a promise to update her after the appointment, anything to distract myself from the nerves building inside me. Then came a gentle knock at the door. I took a deep breath, bracing myself as tears threatened to spill over.

The oncologist entered with a warmth that instantly put me at ease. He explained that my cancer was slow-growing and estrogen and progesterone-fed, meaning it wasn't self-sustaining—it needed estrogen and progesterone to survive. That one word, estrogen, hit me like a gut punch. The flood of emotions—anger, sadness, frustration—rushed back through me. Knowing my cancer was hormone-driven was both comforting and terrifying. Comforting because it wasn't some aggressive, fast-moving force inside me, but terrifying because I had battled hormone issues since 2011. My body had been swimming in estrogen for years.

He reassured me, again and again, that I was in the best-case scenario: early detection, slow growing, highly treatable, and an excellent prognosis. As he spoke, my emotions overwhelmed me, and the tears I had been holding back finally spilled over. Unlike other doctor's visits, where I might have felt embarrassed for crying, here, I felt no shame. He was used to this. My tears were more than fear—they carried stress, relief, gratitude, and hope.

He walked us through everything in detail, even sketching a diagram to show where my cancer was, its type, and what the treatment plan would look like. His recommendation was a lumpectomy, or I could opt for a mastectomy if that is the route I wanted to go, followed by radiation and hormone-blocking medication. But before any decisions could be made, I needed an MRI to give the surgeon a full picture of what we were dealing with. My surgical consultation was set for just a few days later, on July 11, 2024.

Oddly enough, there was a sense of comfort in having a plan—checking off appointments, following the steps, moving forward. It made me feel like I was regaining some control. But one lingering thought tugged at me—I had another trip, this time to California for my mom's birthday. Would I still be able to go? My oncologist assured me that I was cleared to travel, as long as I took precautions—hand washing, sanitizing, and basic common sense. The only thing that could alter my plans was if the surgeon scheduled my surgery beforehand, which didn't seem likely.

Later, when I talked to my mom, the conversation was a blur—one of those talks where you say everything and nothing at the same time. What stood out most was how much I craved normalcy, even in the midst of all this uncertainty. My daughter, who had originally asked not to hear about my appointment until she got home from work because she didn't want to cry at work, changed her mind. She sent me a text and let me know that she didn't want to wait all day wondering about my appointment. I knew it was hard for her to hear, but her texts were as loving and supportive as ever.

I've always known I was lucky to have an incredible family, but my diagnosis brought that truth into sharper focus. It's the little things that mean the most—the way my mom ordered the same Starbucks drink as me from hundreds of miles away, just so we could feel connected, or how my aunt sends surprise flowers, her way of wrapping me in love from afar. The list could go on and on. These quiet, thoughtful gestures remind me that no matter what lies ahead, I'm never walking this path alone.

## Chapter 7

# Facing Fear
## *Unseen Trials*

I had no idea I was claustrophobic—what a surprise that was! As someone who prides herself on being a research queen, I really dropped the ball on this one. My understanding of MRIs was pretty basic: you get an IV for contrast, lie inside a tube, and try to tune out the loud clattering and thumping of the machine. What I didn't anticipate was that, for a breast MRI—at least in my case—I would need to lie face down, positioning my breasts into a rigid device meant to keep them in place. The setup was awkward, elevating my chest in a way that pressed against my ribs, making it difficult to relax or even breathe normally. With my arms stretched above my head, I felt like I was diving into a pool—only this was far from a peaceful plunge.

The technician explained that the procedure would take about 30 minutes, with the contrast injected halfway through. As I was slowly slid into the MRI tube, everything seemed manageable at first. But then, things took a turn. At 5'4" and around 240 lbs., my size suddenly felt painfully obvious. About 80% of the way into the machine, I felt the faintest touch—just a graze—but it was enough to send a shockwave of panic through me. Then it hit me: the machine had brushed against my butt!

Suddenly, heat flushed through me. I was sweating, gasping for breath, heart pounding. I needed out—immediately.

Sensing my distress, the technician asked if I wanted to stop. Yes! As she pulled me back out, I was overwhelmed by a primal fight-or-flight response I had never experienced before. When she gently asked if I wanted to try again, my emotions broke through. I couldn't stop the tears. This MRI was critical for my treatment, yet the thought of going back inside that tube filled me with absolute dread.

The technician suggested I message my surgeon through MyChart to explain my unexpected claustrophobia. She also recommended asking about mild sedatives and scheduling the MRI at a facility with a larger machine. It turned out the machine I had just panicked in had a 55-inch opening, while the hospital had one with a 75-inch opening. That sounded much more doable—if this one was a 55-inch, surely a 75-inch would be better, especially with some medication to help me relax.

My husband had taken time off work to drive me to the appointment. Normally, I'm fiercely independent, so asking for help—even accepting help—felt unnecessary. But at that moment, his support meant everything. After I changed back into my clothes, I texted him to pick me up at the back door since it was closer to where I was at, and the last thing I wanted to do was walk all the way across the building crying. I felt defeated, which seems silly in hindsight, but in that moment, it was all-consuming.

I practically sprinted to the truck, where my husband pulled me into a reassuring hug, promising to be there for the next one. After gathering my thoughts, I called my mom. Like my husband, she was incredibly supportive, but I couldn't shake the embarrassment. Both she and my husband had gone through MRIs before, so why couldn't I?

I messaged my doctor, who responded quickly—she updated the request to go to the hospital for the MRI and prescribed Xanax to ease my anxiety. A sensible solution. Why hadn't we thought of this sooner? Despite the relief, embarrassment still clung to me.

Every appointment felt like another hurdle on this overwhelming journey. Now, on top of processing my diagnosis, I was battling my own mind, wrestling with disappointment in myself. At least I didn't have to complete the MRI before my surgical consultation in two days. But something inside me had cracked. The panic attack had unlocked a flood of anxiety I hadn't known was in me. Just thinking about trying again left me in tears. As if my body wanted to pile on, my premenstrual symptoms and a migraine crashed in, compounding my distress. I spiraled. When I say that I spiraled, I mean I completely broke. My family tried to comfort me, but all I could do was sob, *"I can't do this. I don't want to do this anymore."* Just remembering that moment brings fresh tears. I've never in my life felt so defeated.

My daughter has always had a deep compassion for others—she even keeps blankets and small bags of non-perishable food in her trunk for people in need. But when it comes to seeing me suffer, I think it hits her even harder.

I took a Tylenol PM and crawled into bed, hoping that sleep would bring relief—both physically and emotionally. As I lay there crying in pain and defeat, my daughter gently rubbed my back in the most nurturing way, whispering over and over that everything would be okay, that she was there for me. Her care was so tender, so motherly. I hated that my pain caused her distress. I can't help but wonder if this will leave a lasting mark on her heart. If the roles were reversed—if it were my mom in this state—I know how deeply it would affect me.

The next morning, my mom sent me a text I'll never forget:

*"I'm flying up today. I need to be with you."*

Her words hit me in a way nothing else had. Without my knowledge, my husband had already arranged for her to fly up. Whether it was him, my daughter, or both of them who had made the call—who had told her just how bad things had gotten for me—I wasn't sure. But one thing was clear: I had scared them. I scared myself.

I was terrified, exhausted, and drowning in a sea of misery. But for the first time, a small wave of comfort broke through the fear—my mom was flying in to be with me. She would be by my side and with me at my consultation with the surgeon. And somehow, that made all the difference.

This journey was breaking me in ways I never expected. But it's also revealing just how much love surrounds me. And that, at least, is something to hold on to.

# Chapter 8

# Strength in Vulnerability
## *The Power of Support*

After a solid night's sleep—and with the help of Tylenol PM to ease the aches and relentless migraine—I finally felt a little more like myself. Having my mom there brought comfort I hadn't even realized I needed. Even if there had been no consultation, I know she would have come anyway. She was worried about me. And like the incredible mom she is, she understood that it wasn't just about her being here for me—I needed to be with her, too.

It's strange how deeply we internalize other people's words. I lost count of how many messages I received from family and friends saying things like, *"The next time will be better," "Just focus on getting to your happy place,"* or, *"I'm sorry you're struggling—it was so easy for me."* Some even said, *"Crazy how hard this is for you."* I know none of them intended to be hurtful, but their words weighed on me. Already overwhelmed with emotion, I couldn't help but feel judged—like I was failing at something that should have been easier. It left me feeling not just vulnerable, but somehow pathetic.

Here we were again, heading into another consultation. If there's one thing I dread, it's surgery—there's nothing enjoyable about it, just an unavoidable reality. But sitting in the waiting room with my mom and husband beside me provided some comfort. If this appointment was anything like my last one with the oncologist, I knew I'd be bombarded with information, and my brain might struggle to process it all. Thankfully, I had two extra pairs of ears to help me take it in.

My mom and I are so much alike, especially when it comes to our emotions. We had already been on the verge of tears more times than I could count that day. Through it all, my husband remained steady—he's never tried to change me or make me feel bad for being emotional. Instead, he was my rock, offering strength when I felt weak and a shoulder to cry on. That day, and for many more to come, he was there for both me and my mom.

When the surgeon walked in, her kindness was immediately evident. Some people just radiate warmth, and she was one of them. She carefully explained the procedure: two incisions—one to remove the tumor, another to extract at least one lymph node, and that tiny titanium clip that had been put in when I had my biopsy done. She walked us through the surgery and recovery process, and to my surprise, it didn't sound as terrifying as I had imagined. I reminded myself how grateful I was to be having a lumpectomy rather than a mastectomy. Surgery and recovery are never easy, but I was ready. It had been one month since I first saw those life-altering words in my biopsy results. A month may not seem long, but when you feel like you're carrying a ticking time bomb in your chest, it feels like an eternity. I was eager to have it removed.

I've said it before, and I'll say it again—I'm beyond grateful for my support system. My family has an incredible way of lifting my spirits. My husband surprised me with a box of my favorite macarons. My mom, daughter, and I treated ourselves to pedicures. Even my daughter's close friend stopped by just to hug me and bring me a Starbucks. I felt so incredibly loved. Could I possibly feel more supported than this?

The answer? *Yes*.

Sometimes, the right people walk into your life at just the right moment, bringing a kind of strength and energy that feels almost magical. My daughter works with some truly amazing people, but one woman in particular who we've become close with is someone special. She has a way of making others feel seen, valued, and supported. My daughter mentioned that she was stopping by to drop something off, but we had no idea what was coming.

When she walked in, she was wearing a black shirt with the words *"Support Squad"* across the front, a breast cancer awareness ribbon replaced the a in the word Squad and the hashtag *"#TeamJessica – You Got This!"* The moment my mom and I saw it, we both started crying, which of course made my daughter cry too. The emotions were overwhelming—love, gratitude, disbelief, joy, sadness, hope—all hitting me at once. But she didn't just have a shirt for herself. She had shirts made for my entire family—everyone except my mom, since she had flown up last-minute. And for me, she had something extra special: a pink shirt that read *"Warrior,"* with the ribbon and *"#TeamMe – I Got This!"* underneath.

It was more than just a shirt. It was a symbol of the love and support holding me up, a tangible reminder that I wasn't alone in this fight. But as I held it in my hands, a part of me hesitated—I didn't feel like I had earned it. Warrior. That title belonged to the women in the trenches of stage 4, the ones enduring the brutal battles, the women losing their hair, fighting with everything they had. Compared to them, I didn't feel like a warrior.

Looking back, I understand why women with breast cancer call themselves warriors. This journey is a battle—fought not just in the body, but deep in the heart and mind. In the beginning, I didn't fully feel it; I had no idea what was coming. But now? I've faced it all. And damn right—I *am* a warrior.

CHAPTER 9

# A Sanctuary of Sunshine
## *Home Is Where the Heart Is*

My parents live on a breathtaking 200-acre ranch in Northern California, and when I say it's a little slice of heaven, I mean it with all my heart. Their home is not only beautiful but also incredibly peaceful—the only sounds are the birds chirping and the occasional faint ringing of a cowbell in the distance. They say home is where the heart is, and I feel that deeply. Though I didn't grow up in this house, my heart belongs to my family, which makes their home feel like home to me. I was beyond grateful to have the chance to fly down and soak up the California sun. Sure, it was sunny in Vancouver, Washington, too, but there's something about the California sunshine—it feeds the soul in a way nothing else does. And in that moment, it was exactly what I needed.

We spent my mom's birthday lounging by the pool, which felt like such a gift in itself. Every time I visit, I make sure to see my uncle, his family, and my aunt. Those reunions fill my heart with joy, a reminder of the deep roots and love that hold us all together.

Between our coffee chats and quality time, I took moments for myself—to sit alone, gazing out at the golden California hills, reflecting on life. Those quiet moments were bittersweet. A deep sadness settled over me as I thought about the challenges my family and I were facing with my breast cancer diagnosis. But just as quickly, I was reminded of the immense love that surrounded me—my husband, my kids, my parents, my aunt, my uncle, a few friends. Each of them, in their own way, is already pouring their love and energy into my journey. Their unwavering support was something I would cherish forever.

During that trip, through conversations and introspection, I came to a realization—I was struggling to say the words *"breast cancer"* out loud. Instead, I found myself calling it *"the C word."* I wasn't entirely sure why it felt so difficult to name, but there was an unspoken weight attached to it. A strange feeling of shame, or maybe something that made me feel unclean. Looking back, I no longer feel that way, and I still don't fully understand why I did then.

As I've said from the beginning, I want to share everything—the good, the bad, and the messy. Some of the emotions I've had throughout this journey have felt odd, maybe even dramatic. But none of that matters. What matters is that they were real. I struggled to find stories from people who weren't relentlessly positive, always in "kick cancer's ass" mode. Where were the stories that felt raw and honest, the ones that said, *"This is hard, and sometimes I'm not okay"*?

A dear friend—someone who has been in my life for decades despite living in Alabama and us not having lived in the same state since 2003—offered me words of comfort during one of my lowest moments. She said, *"Never feel bad about feeling sad or angry about what you're going through. Your emotions are valid because this is your journey."*

She was right. I had spent far too much time trying to convince myself that I should be feeling something different, something more "acceptable." But the truth is, every emotion—every tear, every moment of fear, every messy, unexplainable feeling—was valid. And they still are.

I wish I could have stayed in California longer, but my husband, my kids, and my pets were waiting for me at home—they needed me, too. And with my MRI appointment still looming ahead, I knew it was time to return. Even though the trip was short, my heart felt full, grateful for the time I had and the support I received while I was there.

## Chapter 10

# Facing Fear (Again)
## *The MRI Challenge Revisited*

My parents knew how much my last MRI had shaken me, so they decided to fly up to be with me. Their visit was a win-win—my kids got to spend precious time with their grandparents, my husband enjoyed time with his in-laws, and I had the emotional support I desperately needed.

This time, I felt more prepared. I knew what to expect, but the memories of my last attempt were fresh in my mind. The only comfort I had was knowing I'd be in a larger MRI tube and that I had a Xanax to take beforehand. I had never taken Xanax before, but friends assured me it would help keep me calm, making this experience far easier than the last. That was the hope. It was time to face my fears—again.

To keep my stress levels low, we kept things light the night before. We went out for dinner to avoid the hassle of cooking and cleaning –my favorite, Mexican food. Normally, when we have company, I try to take quick showers so that I can spend as much time with them as I can, but this time I indulged in a long, relaxing hot shower, and I went to bed early. Thankfully, my appointment was scheduled for late morning, allowing for a slower, calmer start to the day. My husband took time off work to go with my parents and me. On the way to the hospital, I took the Xanax as instructed, about 20 minutes before we arrived. I didn't feel much of a difference, but at least my anxiety hadn't spiraled out of control. That alone felt like a small victory.

I reassured my husband and dad that they could hang out and chat in the truck. When my mom and I walked into the imaging department, I thought to myself, *"I've got this. We'll be fine!"* As we entered the medical building, I couldn't help but notice my mom's shirt. Remember the *"Support Squad"* shirts our friend had given us? She had shared the Etsy link with my mom, who ordered matching ones for her, my dad, and even my aunt. That day, she proudly wore hers, and it felt like armor—a symbol of strength surrounding me.

But as it turned out, I didn't have it under control after all.

Once we were in the MRI area, my mom took a seat while I changed into the hospital gown, mentally preparing myself for what was to come. The technician asked if I'd had an MRI before, and I explained my last experience, adding that I had taken a Xanax this time in hopes of a different outcome. He asked how long ago I'd taken it, which struck me as an odd question. It made me wonder—was he checking if it had kicked in yet? Because if so, it made sense, it sure didn't feel like it was working.

Still, I tried to stay composed. I took slow, deep breaths and focused on my "happy place" before lying down on the table. I requested a fan, remembering how hot I had felt last time. The technician reassured me that the machine had built-in cooling, and if needed, they'd bring an additional fan closer. The cool air helped, and I managed my breathing well. Taking my brother's advice instead of just thinking about how much I love the ocean, I fully immersed myself into my peaceful beach—the way the warm sand moved beneath my feet with each step as I walked toward the water, the rhythmic crash of the waves, the warmth of the sun gently kissing my skin—I thought, *"Maybe this time will be different."*

But the moment the table slid into the machine, panic gripped me. Before I knew it, the anxiety swelled into full-blown panic, and they had to pull me out of the machine. *Again*!

A flood of emotions washed over me—frustration, disappointment, anger, and ultimately, sorrow. I wasn't just upset with myself, I was heartbroken at the thought of my mom waiting outside, undoubtedly hopeful that this time I'd make it through the MRI. Now, I had to step out and tell her I had failed. *Again*.

Before I left the room, the technician suggested that I contact my surgeon's office to request something stronger than Xanax for my next appointment. I've never liked anesthesia, but at this point, I was desperate enough to consider it—anything to make this easier. I hesitated, then asked if full sedation was an option.

His answer was immediate but kind. *"Unfortunately, no. Since the procedure requires you to be face down, full sedation could interfere with your breathing."*

Just like that, the small flicker of hope vanished as quickly as it had appeared. I swallowed my disappointment, nodding as I tried to steady myself. Taking a deep breath, I gathered what was left of my composure before opening the door.

My mom sat patiently waiting, likely expecting me to emerge victorious. Instead, I stepped out and immediately broke into tears. Without hesitation, she wrapped me in her arms, soothing me the way only a mother can.

*"I couldn't do it,"* I choked out between sobs.

She held me tighter. *"It's okay. We'll try again, and I'll be right there with you."*

In that moment, I felt like a helpless child, wishing she could fix this for me. But this was something I had to conquer on my own.

As we walked outside, my dad and husband sat in the truck, likely deep in conversation about their favorite topics—trucks, guns, home repairs, and ranch life. The moment my husband saw me, he knew. Without a word, he stepped out, wrapped his arms around me, and once again, I broke down.

*"It's okay, babe. I'm here,"* he whispered, echoing my mom's reassurance.

I wanted so badly to believe them, but all I felt in that moment was frustration—frustration at myself, at my body's reaction, at my inability to control this overwhelming unexplainable fear. No amount of comforting words could change the way I felt. But I'll admit, stopping at Starbucks on the way home did help lift my spirits just a little.

As I sipped my peppermint white mocha, I typed out a message to my surgeon's nurse, explaining that the Xanax hadn't worked and asking for a stronger alternative. There was some back-and-forth, and I learned my surgeon was on vacation. The nurse reassured me that she was being updated daily on her patients and that they'd figure something out. In that moment, I held onto a glimmer of hope—hope that next time, I'd make it through.

Not a single person—my husband, my parents, my kids, my family, my friends—made me feel like a failure. The truth is, we are often our own harshest critics, holding ourselves to impossible standards. So if I could offer advice to myself and to anyone facing their own struggles, it would be this: Let go of the need to be perfect. Allow yourself to feel every emotion, even the messy ones. And most importantly, extend yourself the same kindness and grace you would offer to someone you love.

Because at the end of the day, we're all just doing our best. And that's enough.

# Chapter 11

# The Weight of Failed Attempts
## *The Struggle Continues*

The frustration and disappointment refused to fade, lingering like an unwelcome shadow. I felt trapped in an endless cycle of anxiety, fear, and failure. No matter how much I tried to move past it, the weight of those failed MRI attempts pressed down on me. My parents flew home, and life resumed its usual rhythm—but my anxiety and uncertainty stayed. Just the thought of another MRI sent my nerves into overdrive. The knowledge that I had to get through it in order to have surgery only made the pressure feel more suffocating.

My mom's text message to me during this time was a much-needed dose of reassurance. She wrote, *"I know you feel frustrated. Please don't be hard on yourself. You keep trying to do the MRI - you're not a quitter."* Her words resonated deeply with me because they were the truth. I'm not a quitter, and I've been fighting with every ounce of strength I possess. But the thought started to creep in that I might not be strong enough to handle any of this.

Despite my determination, my body betrayed me every time I stepped into that claustrophobic MRI space. I kept telling myself, *"This is ridiculous. I know the machine isn't going to swallow me whole."* But my body didn't care about reason. It reacted as if I was in real, imminent danger, leaving me feeling helpless and frustrated. Looking back, I thought about the times I had told my daughter to "just breathe" when she was having an anxiety attack. I now understood how inadequate those words were and I have apologized to her for that. I had always prided myself on being able to stay calm—I had given birth to two of my three kids without any pain medication, so I knew that I could settle my breathing and calm myself down through pain and fear. So how could I not control whatever was causing my body to panic during the MRI? Once panic takes hold, logic and reason go out the window.

The surgeon's nurse called and let me know that she had put in a prescription for Valium, saying it would be more effective than Xanax. I felt like, *yea right I've heard that before*. One of my friends is a nurse practitioner so I sent her a short message and explained what had been going on and asked her if she thinks that Valium will work better than the Xanax did. She echoed the surgeon's sentiments, telling me that Valium should do the trick. I decided I needed to stack the odds in my favor so I called the imaging department to ask them if they could administer more Valium at the time of my appointment, if needed. They told me they can't do that but that the Valium will likely make me feel a bit sleepy but mostly zoned out during the procedure and that my brain won't process the claustrophobia. Although not what I was hoping to hear, the information brought me some comfort, and I'm grateful for the reassurance that I should be sleepy and zoned out. But the anxiety and fear lingered, a constant reminder that I still need to face this challenge head-on.

The anxiety never truly faded. It clung to me, heavy in my chest—a constant, unrelenting weight. No matter how much I tried to push it down, the fear remained, reminding me that this battle was far from over. I still had to face it. I still had to find a way through.

The stress of knowing this MRI was the next step toward surgery consumed me. Every failed attempt felt like another roadblock, pushing that critical day further and further away. The ticking time bomb inside me grew louder with each passing moment, and no matter how hard I tried to drown it out, I could hear it echoing in my mind.

## Chapter 12

# The Battle of the Third Attempt
### *Conquering the MRI*

The call came—another MRI was scheduled just four days after the last failed attempt. No time like the present to get it over with, right?

When Walgreens notified me that my Valium prescription was ready, I picked it up and asked the pharmacist if she thought it would actually help this time. I explained how the first two attempts had gone, and she reassured me that Valium was commonly prescribed for situations like this—much better suited than Xanax.

Later, I vented to a close friend in Montana, someone who has always been a solid sounding board for me. I told her how frustrating it was not knowing how my body would respond to these medications—how much easier it would be if I just knew what worked for me. She simply replied, *"Hey, it's not a bad thing that you've never needed Xanax or Valium before."*

She was right.

Even though my parents had just flown up for my second MRI, my mom knew how much I was struggling. When she said she'd be there for the next one, she meant it. True to who she is, she booked another flight without hesitation, determined to stand by my side for this third attempt as well.

My dad couldn't make it this time, and I understood. He was in the middle of building an art studio for my mom, tied to the unpredictable schedules of delivery drivers and contractors. But even though he wasn't coming, he still drove my mom to the airport—an hour each way—because that's just who he is.

A part of me couldn't shake the guilt. I felt like I was wasting everyone's time and money just trying to accomplish this one thing. But it wasn't just my mom making sacrifices—my daughter felt my unease and took time off work to be there, offering her emotional support. My husband did the same, stepping away from his own responsibilities to stand by me.

Four people, pausing their lives, rearranging their schedules—all for me. All for another attempt at this dreaded MRI. The weight of their love and support was overwhelming, yet a small voice inside me still whispered, *Do I deserve this much support?*

To say I was anxious would be a massive understatement. I was beyond anxious. I had already failed twice—once believing I could just power through it and once with Xanax in my system. Each attempt only reinforced my fear, locking in feelings of disappointment and shame. This third attempt had to be the last. I *had* to succeed.

Just as instructed, I took the Valium ahead of time. I even skipped my morning coffee for good measure. But as we drove to the medical building, I could feel the anxiety rising anyway. Tears threatened to spill over before we even arrived. My phone was flooded with messages of support—"You've got this," "This time will be better," "I believe in you"—and while I appreciated every single one, I couldn't shake the nagging doubt in my mind.

Thankfully, the drive wasn't long, which left less time for my nerves to spiral out of control. My husband drove the four of us there, and when we checked in, we were told that only two people could accompany me to the back. Being the gentleman he is, my husband let my mom and daughter go while he waited in the front lobby.

As we walked down the hallway toward the dressing room, I kept hoping that the Valium would hit me harder—that I'd be so out of it I'd need help walking. That didn't happen. I felt... maybe a little slower, but not nearly as sedated as I had hoped.

My mom and daughter were dressed in matching *"Support Squad"* shirts—double the strength, double the emotional armor surrounding me. They took their seats outside the dressing room while I stepped inside, grateful for a moment alone. I took my time changing, trying to steady my breathing. The weight of this moment felt unbearable, like an elephant sitting on my chest.

*"This time will be different,"* I repeated in my head. *"Third time's the charm."*

My mind, though, was at war with itself—positive thoughts battling against the deeply ingrained fear that had taken root.

One last deep breath.

I stepped out, hugged my mom and daughter tightly, and walked into the MRI room.

The technician this time was noticeably less friendly than the last one. The air in the room was thick with my anxiety, and everyone could feel it. She asked if I had taken the Valium, then casually remarked that I should be much more relaxed than I was.

No shit, lady. Thanks for stating the obvious.

Right on cue, the tears started. Not just a few rogue ones—full-on, uncontrollable sobbing. Tears of fear, stress, anxiety, disappointment, shame, and embarrassment.

The technician guided me onto the table, and I tried to center myself—slow breaths, happy place, picturing the relief on my family's faces if I could just get through this. But nothing worked. My body trembled, the fear gripping me tighter with every passing second.

Then, she sighed. She actually sighed! And with a hint of impatience, she said, *"You just need to get it done."*

As if I wasn't already trying my hardest. As if I wanted to be trapped in this cycle of fear, forcing my mind and body through hell over and over again. As if I enjoyed locking in these feelings of dread and disappointment.

Her words didn't help—they stung. They dismissed the very real battle I was fighting at that moment, making me feel weak instead of understood.

I made it into the tube.

I did not make it through the MRI.

Between my sobbing and the violent uncontrollable shaking, the technician finally determined that even if I managed to stay inside, the images would be unusable. It wasn't worth continuing.

But instead of compassion, I was met with cold indifference. She wasn't just unsympathetic—she was outright rude. The last technician hadn't been particularly kind, but this one? She made no effort to hide her annoyance.

Through this entire experience, nearly everyone I had encountered had shown me kindness and understanding. Everyone except the MRI technicians at this hospital.

And just like that, my sobs turned from quiet despair to full-on devastation.

The technician, still lacking an ounce of bedside manner, suggested I call my surgeon and let her know the Valium hadn't been enough. She also suggested that I should take one the night before, so that my system would already be in a calmer state by morning and then take another one before my appointment to keep me calm.

Walking to the door felt impossible, like it had suddenly doubled in distance and the door was made of steel. I was about to walk out and face my support squad—once again, defeated. Once again, I had let myself and my family down.

I didn't even try to pull myself together this time. I stepped out, bawling.

My mom and daughter pulled me into their arms, their sadness for me palpable—not disappointment, just pure love and unwavering empathy.

This time, when I stepped into the dressing room to change, I didn't move. I just sat on the bench beside the lockers and let the tears fall. They carried so many emotions—grief, frustration, exhaustion—and not a single one of them was good.

When I finally pulled myself together and got dressed, my mom and daughter linked their arms through mine as we walked toward the waiting room. In that moment, they weren't just beside me—they were holding me up, quite literally my support. I felt like I couldn't even stand on my own, the weight of sorrow pressing down too heavily.

As soon as we reached the waiting room, my husband wrapped me in his arms. He didn't need to say anything—just the quiet, reassuring reminder that I would get through this. Somehow.

But I knew—I couldn't keep doing this. This wasn't going to work.

Like I said before, I don't like to ask for help but I decided to reach out to the breast care center nurse. She had told me before that she'd help however she could, so as soon as we got home, I emailed her, explaining everything I had been through with each attempt. I asked if she had any advice. I was just hoping that she would email me back before the end of the day, since it was a Friday I didn't want to sit with these feelings all weekend.

With my husband back at work, my mom, daughter and I were sitting on the couch talking when my phone rang, just minutes after I sent the email. I answered on speaker phone, and I was so thankful I had reached out.

The breast care center nurse, in her calming, reassuring way, told me something I desperately needed to hear: I didn't *have* to do the MRI. It wasn't a mandatory thing. It had only recently become a part of the standard procedure, and plenty of women had their surgeries without it. Some people simply couldn't do MRIs for various reasons—and that was okay. I wasn't alone.

The feeling of defeat still lingered, but for the first time in weeks, I felt a sense of relief.

Three failed attempts had cemented a new fear within me. I don't know if I'll ever be able to get through an MRI—and honestly, I hope I'm never in a situation where I have to find out.

## Chapter 13

# A Storm Within
## *The Weight of Unseen Wounds*

My mom flew home the next day, and life resumed as normally as possible. On the surface, everything seemed to be clicking along as usual—but I wasn't the same. I felt broken, defeated. It's strange to feel the weight of this diagnosis so deeply, yet look unchanged on the outside. I felt gross, almost dirty, and overwhelmingly disappointed in myself, yet no one could tell just by looking at me that I was going through such a huge struggle. Maybe my family could sense it—they know me so well—but maybe not. I didn't know how to move forward, how to shake these heavy emotions. Stacking on top of the pile of heavy emotions it was almost unbelievable that something as routine as a 30-minute MRI had become such an insurmountable challenge. Even though the breast care center nurse reassured me that the MRI wasn't essential for surgery, I couldn't shake the feeling that I had let everyone down—myself, my family, my surgeon, everyone.

I was genuinely grateful that the breast care center nurse was stepping in to take charge of the situation, reaching out to the surgeon and bridging the gap to find a solution. It wasn't that I didn't want to handle it myself, but she assured me—this is what she does, this is how she helps. When things aren't working and a patient needs extra support, she steps in and makes sure they get it.

I trusted her.

I let her know that the surgeon had been out of town for personal time, so I wasn't sure when she'd be back. She reassured me that she would reach out and that either she or the surgeon would call me within the next few days. Knowing she was on it lifted some of the weight off my shoulders.

This entire experience had been awful, stirring up emotions I didn't know how to process. So many people said things like, *"At least it was caught early,"* and *"You'll be fine."*

And while they weren't wrong, those words only made my feelings feel dismissed, as if they weren't valid. Of course, I was grateful—grateful that it was Stage 1 and not Stage 4, grateful that I only needed radiation and not chemotherapy. I knew I would survive this; there was no doubt about that. But despite all that, I couldn't shake the fear that this journey was going to break me. One thing I know for sure is that early doesn't mean easy.

## CHAPTER 14

# Anchored by Support
### *Facing the Unknown Together*

Even though my mom had just flown back to California a few days earlier, she was back in Vancouver once again—this time to go with me to my radiation oncology consultation. I wasn't sure what to expect. In my mind, radiation felt ominous, like I'd be lying there while laser beams flooded my body with something I couldn't see but might somehow feel. Normally, I make it a point to gather as much information as possible, but at this stage, I was so overwhelmed. There was simply too much to process, so I hadn't even researched radiation beforehand. Instead, we stepped into the unknown together.

My husband had been by my side at nearly every appointment, but this time, it was just my mom and me. I can't remember if she was wearing her *Support Squad* shirt, but knowing her, she probably was.

As we pulled into the parking lot and we saw the signs for Radiation Oncology Patient Parking, it felt surreal. *How was it even possible that I needed to be here?* I didn't belong here. Pushing down my nerves, I put on a brave face and walked in. The receptionist was so warm and friendly that it almost caught me off guard. How could a place that carried such a heavy weight feel so light and welcoming?

While waiting, my mom and I noticed a small bookshelf filled with books for patients to borrow. Curious, I asked if they were meant to be read only in the office or if they could be taken home. The receptionist smiled and said they were there for whatever felt right. I had no plans to take one—my mind was at capacity—but I did know an author whose books I could bring in for other patients. Spoiler alert: that author is my mom.

The radiation oncologist was kind, informative, and reassuring. He walked me through the process and explained that I'd need to practice taking a deep breath and holding it for 30 seconds. He suggested practicing while lying on the floor since a bed or couch would provide too much give, making it easier than it would be during treatment. He was right—it made a huge difference. 30 seconds doesn't sound like very long at all but at least for me, 30 second deep breath holds was pushing my limit.

He explained that with breast cancer—especially when it involves the left breast—there's a risk that radiation can cause some scar tissue to form on both the lungs and the heart. While there's no real way to prevent scarring on the lungs, there was a technique to help protect my heart. By holding my breath during treatment, my lungs would expand just enough to shift my heart slightly out of the radiation field. That was all I needed to hear. If something as simple as a deep breath could help shield my heart, I was fully on board.

Of course, radiation comes with other side effects. We all know it's not harmless—after all, even at the dentist, they leave the room when they take an X-ray. My radiation oncologist was very transparent about what to expect. He explained that the tissue in my left breast would change permanently—it would become firmer due to internal scarring. Down the road, when gravity naturally takes its toll, my breasts wouldn't quite match anymore. The left would stay firmer and sit differently than the right. They would also be keeping a close eye on my ribs through regular imaging, watching for any signs of radiation-related fractures.

It was a lot to take in. That initial consultation gave me a clear picture of the physical impact this treatment would have—and just how real things were about to get.

From that moment on, I made it a habit to practice regularly—not just lying on the floor but in the little moments of my day. Driving in my car. While stirring dinner on the stove. While I was doing my makeup. Every breath was a quiet act of preparation, a small but meaningful way to take control of what I could.

Walking out of the appointment, I felt lighter. I wasn't looking forward to radiation, but I felt more prepared. Every person we encountered had been incredibly kind and positive, which made all the difference.

## Chapter 15

# Fractured Normalcy
## *Living in Two Worlds*

My mom flew back home, again, and I was grateful for the time we spent together. After my appointment, we made a stop at Hobby Lobby and Starbucks—simple moments that I truly cherished. One of the strangest feelings had been trying to go about normal life while carrying the weight of this diagnosis. It's as if I was living in two realities at once—feeling like I had a ticking time bomb inside me while also experiencing happiness, feeling both normal and different all at once. It's confusing, surreal, and impossible to fully make sense of.

I had been looking forward to seeing the *movie It Ends With Us* since I had read the book. My husband was in Seattle for work so I decided to go on my own. Don't get me wrong, I would have preferred to go with someone but I was going on a Friday morning afterall, the people who would go with me were working.

I had never been to a movie by myself before. Come to think of it, I don't think I've ever gone out to dinner alone either—though I have spent time at a coffee shop solo. But this was different.

To my surprise, I actually enjoyed it. There was something peaceful about sitting in the theater alone, completely immersed in the story. An added bonus? It was a 9 a.m. showing, so I was literally the only person there.

As I walked out of the movie and made my way from the theater into the main area of the mall, I barely noticed the play area filled with moms and their little ones. I remembered those days, but my mind was elsewhere. I was almost to the doors when I heard a familiar voice call my name.

I turned around—and there was my husband.

He had just driven back from Seattle. Unlike me, who would have slept in and taken my time getting on the road, he had gotten up early and headed straight home. He felt bad that

I had gone to the movie alone and wanted to take me out for coffee and macarons—a sweet, thoughtful gesture.

I had genuinely enjoyed seeing the movie by myself, but I understood why he thought it was a little sad. In 27 years of marriage, I had never once gone to a movie alone.

Since we had driven separately, I followed him across the street to Sweet Touch Café—the place with the best macarons.

During the movie, I got a call from a Syracuse New York number—yet another spam call, or so I assumed. I didn't think twice about it until I checked my voicemail. My stomach dropped when I heard the message—it was the surgeon. She was still out of town and calling from her personal cell phone. She mentioned that she had spoken with her nurses, the breast care center nurse and reviewed the latest updates. Immediately, a wave of anxiety hit me. I couldn't shake the fear that she would be disappointed in me. I had been consumed by this strange, nagging worry about letting people down, something I had never struggled with before. Even worse, I feared she would tell me that it was imperative that I had the MRI and needed to try it a fourth time.

I told my husband about the missed call and voicemail, and before we left the café, he hopped into my car while I called her back. It had only been about 20 minutes, but the call went straight to voicemail.

I left a message, letting her know I'd be available for the rest of the day, then immediately fell into the cycle of obsessively watching my phone, as if it were a lifeline.

My husband got back in his truck, and as we drove home separately, we stayed on the phone, talking about his work trip and my movie. It felt normal—almost. We were both just waiting, hoping, willing the surgeon to call back.

Hours later, when she called back, I took a deep breath and braced myself for what she might say. But instead of disappointment, I was met with reassurance.

She told me there was no real benefit in putting me through another MRI—that it was okay that I hadn't been able to complete it. While MRIs provide detailed images and a full scope of the area, she didn't believe it should come at the expense of my mental health. And with each failed attempt, that cost was only growing. She was comfortable moving forward without it and someone from her office would be reaching out soon.

Relief washed over me. For the first time in weeks, I felt like I could finally exhale.

This was really happening. Things were finally moving forward.

A few days later, some longtime friends came to visit for the day. It's funny how small the world can feel sometimes. We first met years ago when they were stationed at the same Air Force base as my husband, and now, even though they live on the Oregon coast, we still find ways to reconnect.

We spent the day at the Vancouver waterfront—laughing over lunch, walking along the Columbia River, soaking up the sunshine, and catching up on life. Days like these have always been special, but now, they feel even more precious—a welcome escape from the relentless weight of my diagnosis. We talked about it briefly, acknowledging it without letting it define the day. That balance felt important. Cancer was a part of my life now, but it wasn't all of it. Not today. Today was about friendship, connection, and the simple joy of being together.

## CHAPTER 16

# The Ticking Clock
## *Life Moves Forward, But So Does the Fear*

As I've said before, it's strange to carry on with normal life while navigating all these changes. Our oldest son and his girlfriend, who live in Missouri, were flying out to visit us on August 20, 2024. Whenever they visit, we make the most of every moment. Living in the Pacific Northwest means endless opportunities—stunning sights to see, trails to hike, and restaurants to try. Our days would be packed.

I got a call from the nurse at the breast care center. She explained that I needed to go in the next day for a Savi Scout implant. The procedure was similar to the biopsy—they would use an ultrasound to locate the exact spot and implant a reflective beacon. During surgery, the surgeon would use this beacon to precisely locate the tumor and remove as little healthy tissue as possible.

Then the next call was to schedule my surgery. The moment I saw the number on my phone, my stomach sank. I felt like I was going to be sick, yet at the same time, I was impatient to get it over with. I just wanted this ticking time bomb out of me! There was this overwhelming feeling, almost like I had something strapped to my heart, slowly causing damage the longer it stayed. Of course, it was figurative—but it didn't feel that way.

Once the reality of surgery set in, I found myself torn. I was ready, but I also didn't want it to overshadow my son's visit. Thankfully, my surgery was scheduled for the day he and his girlfriend were leaving. It worked out, in a way—most of the last day of a trip is spent packing and preparing to head home anyway.

Every day is this strange dichotomy—good and bad, happy and sad, excitement and fear. It's surreal. Seeing my son is incredibly special. I only get to be with him twice a year, so his visit is all I wanted to focus on. But no matter how much I tried, my diagnosis was still there, weaving itself into every part of my life.

Their visit would be a welcome distraction—the perfect sendoff before I finally get this damn ticking time bomb out of me.

I couldn't help but wonder what surgery would be like. Back in 2011, I had a breast augmentation, and the recovery was moderately difficult. Then, in 2019, I had my breast implants removed, and that recovery was surprisingly much easier. Now, I was facing yet another surgery—but this time, it was different. Of course, surgery meant anesthesia, and I hate anesthesia.

With my brain finally able to process more information, I went into research mode, Googling everything I could about the procedure and, more importantly, the recovery. The surgery itself was in the hands of my surgeon, but the healing? That was on me—and my family. Over and over, I came across recommendations for soft, front-closing bras, preferably with zippers. That seemed like an easy thing to prepare for, so I ordered a few online. The reviews said they'd be helpful not just for surgery but for radiation later on, too.

When it came to pain management, I knew I didn't want to rely on heavy pain medication if I could help it. I hoped Tylenol would be enough, but only time would tell.

## Chapter 17

# A Circle of Strength
## *Wrapped in Love on Surgery Day*

I could write an entire book about my family—their unwavering support, their love, their presence through every moment—but that isn't what this book is about. Our visit with our son and his girlfriend was incredible, and as an added bonus, my parents flew in for my surgery, allowing them to spend a day with them, too. We all went to play miniature golf at a beautiful course nestled in the trees in Happy Valley, Oregon. It was peaceful, almost like a little escape. Afterward, we enjoyed dinner at a Mexican restaurant. Knowing I wouldn't be able to eat after midnight, I fully indulged. My heart felt full, my spirit momentarily light.

On the drive home from miniature golf and dinner, I got a text from my aunt, a video. She was wearing her Support Squad shirt, and her message was the sweetest, most genuine expression of love. She spoke about strength, about pushing through even the hardest days, and about how much she loves me. It took me several times to watch it all the way through—each time, tears welled up in my eyes, and by the halfway point, I was crying. For some reason, vulnerability feels even more raw in a video. I admire her courage to record and send such an emotional video, and I will cherish it forever.

It felt like surgery day took forever to arrive. From my first abnormal mammogram to this moment it had only been three months. Three months sounds like a long time in hindsight, but in the moment, it felt relentless—fast, but never fast enough. The best way I can describe this journey is like being caught in the unforgiving waves of the Atlantic, each one crashing over me before I can catch my breath. Just as I rise, gasping for air, another wave pulls me under.

The morning of surgery, I drove to my parents' hotel to pick them up. Lounging, sipping coffee, and pretending to be relaxed wasn't an option, so I welcomed the task. When my parents stepped outside, hand in hand like they always are, both wearing their "Support Squad" shirts, my heart swelled. I quickly grabbed my phone and snapped a picture. It was such a simple gesture, yet it made me emotional—happy and sad all at once. Their love and support were unwavering, and now they were silently telling the world what they were standing behind.

Before heading to the hospital, I hugged my son and his girlfriend tightly, telling them how much I loved them. They planned to stop by briefly once I was in recovery before heading to the airport, but I didn't want to risk missing the chance for a real goodbye. Bedside hugs are never as good as a true embrace.

Here we go.

My husband and daughter both took the day off work, and our youngest stayed home from school. My mom and husband came to the hospital with me while the rest of the family stayed at home. It helped to divide and conquer—everyone was on edge with anticipation and worry. Once we arrived and checked in, the weight of reality pressed down on me. I wanted to run, to cry, to scream—to do anything but be here. One by one, the nurses, my surgeon, a radiologist, and the anesthesiologist came in. The efficiency of the process was impressive, the only unpredictability being the surgery before mine. And, of course, there was a delay—which delayed my surgery by two hours.

My first thought? *I'm already starving.* My second thought was *I won't get to see my son and his girlfriend before they leave.* I was beyond grateful I hadn't left anything to chance and had given my son extra love before heading out that morning.

I know I've said it before, but I hate surgery. Everything about it. The atmosphere, the waiting, the entire process—it sends my anxiety into overdrive. The delay gave my daughter time to bring my son and his girlfriend to the hospital for a short visit, which I deeply appreciated. They sat with us for a little while, and though I heard the conversation around me, I wasn't fully present. My mind was drowning in anxiety, my ears ringing with the hum of my own thoughts. Still, even one extra hug made their visit worth it.

Shortly after they left, it was time. I hugged my husband and mom goodbye, my voice thick with unspoken emotions. As the nurse wheeled me away, I fought to keep my tears in check, but when I saw my mom's eyes full of tears, mine spilled over. The ride to the operating room felt long, though it probably wasn't. The nurse made small talk, asking about my kids and their ages—an attempt at distraction. But the moment she pressed the button to open the doors to the operating room, my heart pounded.

The routine began: Verify my name, my date of birth, and the procedure I was having done. Then the dreaded transfer from the hospital bed to the surgical table. It's strange how heavy gravity feels in that moment. I could feel the panic creeping in, that familiar fight-or-flight response growing stronger. I told the nurse I was getting anxious—*really* anxious. Within moments, she gave me something to calm me down. Relief washed over me before the full panic could take hold.

Then, nothing.

The next thing I knew, something cold pressed against my lips—ice. A gentle, calming voice followed. *"Hey, Jessica, I'm just giving you some ice to help wake you up."* I could hear her, but my body lagged behind, sluggish and unresponsive. She kept speaking, her words coaxing me back. *"It's time to wake up, Jessica." "Are you ready to wake up now?"*

As my awareness sharpened, she explained that they'd been trying to wake me for about 30 minutes. The ice was a trick to jolt my senses. Time felt warped, as if everything had frozen in place. How long had surgery been? Was my son already back in Missouri? The first words out of my mouth were, *"What time is it?"*

The nurse laughed and told me. I explained that my son was flying home, and I had no idea how long I'd been under. Surgery has a way of making time feel like it just... disappears.

As I became more alert, they wheeled me back to my

room. My mom and husband were right there, waiting, just as they had been before I left. Relief settled in my chest—relief that the surgery was over, that I had made it through, that I was no longer carrying that tiny 10mm cancerous tumor inside me. But then came fear. Fear of the pain that was coming. Fear of what was next. Fear of the unknown.

But in that moment, one thing was clear: I was cancer-free. That little cancerous tumor—the one that had hijacked my life, my thoughts, my peace—was finally gone.

## Chapter 18

# Right Place, Right Time
## *The Unexpected Blessing of Perfect Timing*

I often think about how life's biggest moments happen at either the most inconvenient times or with uncanny perfect timing. For me, my diagnosis fell into the latter.

My youngest son was on summer break. My husband's hybrid work schedule meant he could be home more. My daughter, with years at her job, had the flexibility to take time off. My parents, now retired, were just a short hour-and-a-half flight away. I can't imagine how much harder this would've been if it were the middle of the school year, if my husband had a rigid in-office job, or if we still lived in Missouri. My parents wouldn't have been able to fly back and forth as often, and I would have felt so much more isolated.

And what if I had been working? I feel incredibly fortunate that I don't—I've been living my stay-at-home mom life and I was more grateful for that than ever before.

I'm also relieved we're not in Missouri. My mother-in-law had breast cancer there a decade ago, and her experience was vastly different. She found out through a letter in the mail—I got a call from the compassionate breast care center nurse. Not to say her medical team didn't do what was necessary, but I know, without a doubt, that the care I've received here in Vancouver had been far superior.

## Chapter 19

# The Support Network
### *Balancing Love and Burden*

I'm a natural nurturer. Taking care of others, making sure they feel loved and supported—it's instinctual for me. But being nurtured? That's a different story. It doesn't come naturally, and accepting help makes me feel like a burden. Still, I was grateful that I wasn't in severe pain—just discomfort. Tylenol was enough to manage it during the day, and Tylenol PM helped me sleep at night. Though sleep itself was a challenge. I'm a side sleeper—a left-side sleeper—and that wasn't going to happen for a while.

Some things were manageable, but others were hard. Simple tasks suddenly felt monumental—putting my hair in a ponytail, pulling on a shirt, washing my hair, anything that required me to lift my left arm.

And then, there was the first shower!

It was awful. My husband had to help me undress and get into the shower, which already felt humbling. I ended up showering in the surgical bra they sent me home in because the moment he undid the Velcro, the weight of my own breasts without support made me nauseous. The pain was unbearable. The whole experience was a disaster—undressing, trying to wash my hair, and then the realization that my surgical bra was now soaked, meaning it had to come off anyway. Thankfully, I had ordered those front-zip bras online, and with careful maneuvering, we managed to slide me into a dry one as quickly as possible.

It's shocking how much energy a simple shower drained from me. I felt completely depleted afterward.

Despite the physical challenges, the love and support surrounding me was overwhelming in the best way. Flowers arrived from my aunt, my husband's work, and a friend stopped by to drop flowers off too. My parents sent an Edible Arrangement. Cards filled with kind words and encouragement filled the space around me. Their support was palpable and proof that I wasn't in this alone.

I only needed my husband's help for two days to shower, and my daughter took over my hair for a few days, pulling it into a high ponytail or bun, just to keep it out of my face for the day. It took three days before I could dress myself, and when I finally managed to do it on my own, it felt like I had conquered Mt. Everest. A seemingly small victory, but a monumental one in this journey.

Even now, it all feels surreal. I had cancer. I have cancer? I'm not even sure at what point someone is considered "cancer free". But I did feel lighter knowing the tumor was gone. I had promised myself I'd be real about this entire experience, and the truth is—having that tumor inside me made me feel disgusting. Dirty. Shameful. I know that's irrational, but it's how I felt. Having it out helped, but some of those feelings still lingered.

Had I lived healthier? Managed my weight better? Pushed my doctors harder?

The "should-haves" and "could-haves" looped endlessly in my mind.

But the reality is—I was here. Healing. Moving forward. That had to count for something.

## Chapter 20

# Silent Battles
## *The Loneliness Within Support*

Support is something worth pausing to acknowledge. I will always sing the praises of the people in my life who have made me feel seen and cared for. But support and loneliness are two very different things. Even with a strong support system, I still felt alone.

I chose not to join support groups, not because I didn't appreciate the idea, but because I was afraid—afraid of forming connections through trauma, afraid of meeting someone with a terminal diagnosis, afraid of encountering relentless optimism that felt out of reach. Instead, I found myself stuck in a strange limbo, feeling like I wasn't "cancery" enough to seek help or sympathy. It's a difficult space to exist in, carrying the weight of a diagnosis while hearing people tell me to be grateful it was caught early—all while feeling like I'm silently screaming underwater, desperate for someone to truly see my struggle and say, *It's okay.*

One of the best things a friend told me was that whatever I feel—fear, anger, sadness, gratitude, exhaustion—is valid. That reminder has been a lifeline, something I repeat to myself often. I am an emotional person, and I am neither ashamed nor embarrassed by that. Maybe some people could handle this diagnosis better than I have, maybe not. But from the very beginning, I promised myself I would do whatever it took to protect my peace and limit unnecessary stress.

No matter how much love surrounded me, the journey still felt lonely.

## Chapter 21

# Behind the Smile
## *The Burden of Hidden Suffering*

Healing takes time—there's no way to speed it up, but there are certainly ways to slow it down. I hate feeling incapable, so I made sure to push myself, but never beyond my limits. At my two-week post-op appointment, I mentioned to my surgeon that my breast felt unbearably heavy. Without the support of a bra, the discomfort was overwhelming.

She explained that I had a sizable hematoma. A hematoma is essentially a collection of blood that pools outside of the blood vessels, usually caused by trauma or surgery. In my case, it formed as a result of the procedure, where small blood vessels had likely bled into the surrounding tissue, creating a firm, swollen, and tender mass. Unlike a simple bruise that disperses on its own fairly quickly, a hematoma takes longer to break down and be reabsorbed by the body.

My surgeon reassured me that, while uncomfortable, this wasn't uncommon and would resolve with time. To help speed up the healing process, she recommended using a heating pad regularly, as warmth increases circulation and encourages the body to gradually absorb the trapped blood. So that's exactly what I did—constantly.

As I focused on physical healing, I was also on edge, waiting for the oncologist to call. After the surgery, the tumor was sent to pathology for further testing. Since it measured 10mm, they also ran an Oncotype DX test to determine whether radiation alone would be enough or if chemotherapy might be necessary. When I first met with the oncologist, he reassured me that chemo wasn't even on the table—*"It's small, it's early, don't worry!"* But now, with the slight size discrepancy, it was suddenly a possibility. Had the tumor been larger than they originally thought? Had it grown between the ultrasound and the surgery? I didn't ask, and honestly, I didn't want to know. They said it was slow-growing, and that's all I needed to hear.

The most frustrating pattern in this journey is the cycle of urgency and waiting—hurry up, wait, hurry up, wait. Everything happens so fast, rushing from one step to the next, only to be met with long, anxious pauses before the next piece of the puzzle falls into place. The waiting is suffocating.

Physically, my recovery was easier than I had feared. The first few days were rough—sleeping was uncomfortable and awkward—but my body adjusted. It's incredible how resilient we are, how quickly our bodies mend themselves. If only our emotions healed as fast. While my body was on track, emotionally, I was unraveling. But that was mine to carry. I didn't want to place the weight of my sadness on anyone else.

My mother-in-law and father-in-law drove up from Northern California to spend a few days with us, and the timing couldn't have been better. I was healing well, feeling more like myself, and even able to get out and enjoy the sunshine.

Since my husband and I have explored many beautiful hiking spots, we decided to take them to Ridgefield National Wildlife Refuge—a stunning, peaceful place. The fresh air, the warmth of the sun, and the simple act of walking together made for a perfect day. We had easy, flowing conversations, and I deeply appreciated the quality time. Even more so, I appreciated that while my cancer journey wasn't ignored, it also wasn't the center of every discussion. It was a welcome break—just a normal day, spent with family, surrounded by nature.

CHAPTER 22

# Beyond the Fear
## *Finding Strength in Answers*

A few days passed before I received a call from the oncology office to schedule a video call with my oncologist to discuss my Oncotype DX test results. This test had been looming in the back of my mind for weeks, giving me plenty of time to research it. While some of the scientific explanations I found online were difficult to digest, the Oncotype DX test itself was relatively straightforward. It evaluates the activity of specific genes in a breast cancer tumor to determine the likelihood of recurrence and whether chemotherapy would provide any significant benefit. Since I have early-stage, hormone receptor-positive, HER2 negative breast cancer, this test was crucial in guiding my treatment plan.

The scoring system ranges from 0 to 100; Low risk where chemo is likely not needed is a score of 0 - 25 and high risk where chemo is likely needed is a score of 26 - 100.

During my call with my oncologist, I felt an overwhelming sense of relief—no chemotherapy was needed! My score came back as 16—closer to the cutoff than I would have liked, but still low enough that chemo wouldn't provide significant additional benefit.

However, he had some concerns about my surgical margin. Ideally, they prefer a 2mm clear margin, but mine was only 1mm. He needed to consult with my radiation oncologist to determine if this was sufficient or if another surgery would be necessary. Wanting an answer as soon as possible, he attempted to call the radiation oncologist while we were still on the video call. It went to voicemail so he left him a detailed message.

By some stroke of luck my radiation oncologist called back before our video chat ended. After reviewing my case, he confirmed that he was comfortable with the margin. Instead of another surgery, he would add four additional "boost" radiation treatments to my plan. The relief that washed over me was indescribable—no chemo and no second surgery!

My oncologist then outlined the next steps: I would move forward with radiation, begin taking Tamoxifen, a hormone-blocking medication, and later discuss ovarian suppression once radiation was complete. He let me know that my radiation oncologist would make the decision if I would remain on Tamoxifen during radiation or pause until it was completed.

Remember those awful premenopausal symptoms I deal with every month? I asked him if the hormone blocker would prevent them from happening. He said it should stop them from happening. YES! That was music to my ears. I was beyond tired of dealing with the same debilitating pain month after month.

I hadn't fully grasped just how much the fear of chemotherapy had been weighing on me. Of course, I dreaded the thought of losing my hair, but it was more than that—it was the symbolic weight of chemo that terrified me. It felt like a threshold between "having cancer" and "fighting cancer" in a way that was too overwhelming to process. My thoughts had been constantly swinging between "I can do this, I'm strong enough" to "I can't take any more, I'm already broken." Now, at least, I could breathe knowing that chemotherapy was no longer part of my journey.

My aunt sent me the most beautiful, cheerful bouquet—a vibrant mix of bright yellow flowers. Tucked inside was a card that read, *"So happy to hear NO chemo! Best news so far."* Her thoughtful gesture filled me with warmth, another tangible reminder of the love and support surrounding me.

CHAPTER 23

# The Rising Tide
## *The Unrelenting Waves of Emotions*

Things were moving forward, and my healing was progressing well. The hematoma remained, feeling just as large as before, and my breast was covered in deep, dark bruises that looked as painful as they felt. But overall, I was recovering. Then, the phone rang—it was the radiation office.

They told me I needed to schedule my "simulation appointment." Simulation? I had no idea what that meant, so I asked. The scheduling nurse explained that I'd need to come in so they could create a mold for me to lie in during each treatment. Then she casually mentioned they'd also be doing tattoos.

Wait—tattoos? Like, actual permanent tattoos?

"Yep," she confirmed. "Just small dots, four of them."

My mind spun as she went on to explain that these weren't done with a tattoo gun but rather with a simple stick-and-poke method. Still, the idea of having permanent marks on my body, a reminder I'd see every day, made my heart break just a little more.

When she called, I was out walking with my husband. Even though it was a short walk, it suddenly felt like I was trekking ten miles uphill. All I wanted to do was get home and start Googling everything—radiation simulation, radiation tattoos, anything that could prepare me for what was coming. But I also wasn't about to let cancer steal this moment. The sun was shining, a rare treat in the Pacific Northwest in late fall, and I wasn't going to let my thoughts drown me in fear. So, we finished our walk, making small talk about anything but cancer.

The moment I got home though, I rushed to my computer. Google search: *What do radiation tattoos look like?* Click. *View images.*

What the heck?! Actual dot tattoos.

My heart sank. The idea of having permanent tattoos on my chest hit me hard. I was already carrying physical reminders—scars from my lumpectomy and lymph node removal—and while I'm not as focused on appearance as I once was, the thought of adding more lasting marks felt overwhelming. These weren't just dots of ink; they were symbols of everything I'd been through, and they'd be with me forever. I was still trying to process that reality when I found myself typing into the search bar: What is a radiation simulation?

And then I saw it—*M-R-I*.

Panic hit me like a freight train. My entire body tensed, my breathing became shallow, and the tears came fast and hard—not just a few stray drops, but full-on, uncontrollable sobbing. I remember sending my mom audio messages, my voice breaking under the weight of my emotions. I can only imagine how difficult it must have been for her to decipher my words through the tears.

An MRI? No one had mentioned an MRI. Why didn't the radiation oncologist tell me this during my consultation? My fear took over, gripping me in a way I hadn't felt in a while.

How was I going to do this? How was I going to get through this?

Will I ever get over the trauma of those failed MRI attempts? I honestly don't know. Even as I write this, just thinking about it makes my heart race and anxiety creep in. It's frustrating because I feel so silly for having this level of anxiety about MRI's. But what's even more confusing is that I can't pinpoint *why* my body had such an extreme reaction.

It wasn't fear of getting stuck. It wasn't the machine closing in on me. It wasn't even the loud noises. And yet, the moment I was in that tube, my body rebelled in a way I couldn't control.

Would it have been different if I could've done the scan lying on my back? Maybe. But now, no matter what, those past experiences are burned into my memory. They won't just disappear. I can't ignore them, and I can't simply push through as if they never happened.

Chapter 24

# The Weight of Worry
## *Easing the Fear Through Answers*

I let a few days pass, but the simulation appointment was still weighing heavily on my mind. The uncertainty gnawed at me, so I decided to call the radiation oncology office to get more information. My biggest question: *Is an MRI involved?*

The receptionist, just as kind as I remembered from my consultation, assured me she would speak with a nurse about my concerns and have someone reach out to me soon. Thankfully, I didn't have to wait long. A nurse called back, her voice warm and reassuring. She immediately put my mind at ease—*the simulation is done with a CT scan, not an MRI*.

That was a relief, but a small knot of anxiety still lingered. I had never had a CT scan either, and while I knew it was different from an MRI, I also knew there were some similarities. I shared my past experiences with panic and my worries about the scan. She listened patiently and suggested that I come in before my appointment to see the machine and get a feel for it. If the panic set in again, she said she would talk to the radiation oncologist about prescribing a mild sedative for my simulation appointment.

A couple of days later, I walked into the radiation oncology office, feeling a little ridiculous for even needing this reassurance. Surely, I was the only patient making such a big deal about this. It was embarrassing, but I pushed that feeling aside—I needed peace of mind more than I needed to avoid embarrassment.

That's when I met the kindest radiation therapist. She would be one of the radiation therapists who would be overseeing my simulation and treatments. From the moment she introduced herself, I knew I was in good hands. Calling her "kind" doesn't even do her justice. She was patient, understanding, and completely nonjudgmental. She even showed me a tiny dot tattoo on her thumb, explaining that she got it just so she could show nervous patients exactly what to expect. If she hadn't pointed it out, I wouldn't have even noticed it.

By the end of my visit, I felt confident about the CT scan—so much better than I ever felt about an MRI. I knew I could handle this.

Looking back, I am so glad I spoke up and voiced my concerns. If I've learned anything through this journey, it's this: *advocate for yourself.* Ask questions. Seek reassurance. Get the answers you need. Peace of mind is worth it.

CHAPTER 25

# The Crimson Wing
*Finding Strength in Unexpected Symbols*

Life felt heavy at every step of this journey. My daughter was turning 20, and all she wanted was a trip to the zoo. On one hand, I was still recovering, drained of energy, and not feeling 100%, but on the other hand, I love the zoo. Well, I have a love-hate relationship with it—I feel for the animals living in captivity, yet I love seeing animals I'd likely never have the chance to see in the wild. Despite my exhaustion, I knew we had to go. Not just because I love animals, but because I love seeing my kids happy. So, with a last-minute plan, my daughter, my youngest son, and I headed to the Portland Zoo.

I've always had a soft spot for flamingos. They remind me of my mom, who loved them when I was growing up, and I've always been drawn to their beautiful color. During my healing, I watched a documentary from Disney's Disneynature collection called Crimson Wing. In it, they shared the definition of flamingo— *"Phoeni•cop•ter•us, the Latin name for flamingo means Crimson Wing. The flamingo is said to be the inspiration for the crimson-winged phoenix, the ancient symbol of transformation and rebirth. At the end of its life, the phoenix is consumed by fire, only to rise again from the ashes."*

That struck a deep chord in me. This was me—transforming into my new reality, a rebirth of who I was becoming. I had been through the fire of this diagnosis, and now, I was emerging from the ashes. It gave me an odd sense of empowerment. *I've got this.* I would use this experience to help others who might need strength through their own hardships.

We stopped to watch the flamingos for a while, admiring a tiny baby flamingo—a flaminglet. The kids had fun wandering through the zoo, watching the animals. My daughter, a huge polar bear fan, lit up when she saw one playing on a mound of grass with a big ball. My son, in a rare display of teenage silliness, stretched his arms out in front of a sign that read, *What is your wingspan?* His wingspan matched that of a bald eagle, which he thought was pretty cool.

Later that night, we had birthday cake—well, everyone except me since it wasn't gluten-free. I had picked up the cake the day before, feeling so clever about the wording I'd requested: *Goodbye teens, hello twenties!* But when I snapped a picture of my daughter holding the cake, we all burst into laughter. Somehow, the cake actually read *Goodbye tweens*! None of us had noticed—not when I picked it up, not when I sent a picture to my mom, not until that very moment. It was a perfect, unintentional joke to end the day.

It had been a good day.

## CHAPTER 26

# A Fortress of Love
## *Strength in Those Who Stand Beside Me*

I still had the hematoma, so I had a quick conversation with my radiation oncologist about it. He suggested following up with the surgeon to ensure it didn't need to be drained. He reassured me that when I came in for my simulation appointment, we could go over what the surgeon said, and he would also do an exam himself.

My mom was back again—surely she is earning frequent flyer miles at this point. Her unwavering support fills my heart, and I can't imagine going through this without her by my side.

That day, I had two back-to-back appointments. First, a follow-up with my surgeon and then across the street to see the radiation oncologist. My husband joined us for the appointment with the surgeon, where she confirmed that I still had a hematoma—just slightly smaller than a fist. *A fist! That's huge.* She reassured me that my body would continue to absorb it, though it could take weeks or even months. Her advice was to continue to use a warm compress a few times a day to promote blood flow and aid healing. Otherwise, everything looked good—no signs of complications, no additional follow-ups needed.

Afterward, my husband had somewhere he had to be but he left me in capable supporting hands with my mom. We drove across the street to the radiation oncology office. Even just parking in that lot felt heavy, and I could sense that my mom felt it too. This journey had been hard on her, and this place only deepened the weight. It's strange how certain buildings seem to carry their own gravity, making every step toward them feel heavier.

My radiation oncologist wasn't overly concerned about the hematoma. He echoed the surgeon's advice about using a warm compress but told me to stop once radiation began, as my skin would be compromised. He explained that my body's healing priorities would shift during treatment, likely slowing the absorption of the hematoma. Still, he'd be monitoring it closely.

Then, it was time for the simulation appointment. In the CT room, we watched a short video explaining how the radiation machine works and what to expect during treatment. I remember feeling the need to put on a brave face. This was already so hard, and I didn't want to add to my mom's worries. If I let myself fall apart, I knew she'd want to scoop me up and shelter me under her protective mom-wing, but that wasn't real life.

The radiation therapist I had met before, guided us through the process. When it was time for the next step, my mom had to return to the waiting room. Before she left, I asked her to take a picture of me standing next to the CT machine to send to my daughter—proof that I was okay, ready to take this on. That picture felt like more than just a photo; it was a reminder to both of us that I was strong.

As my mom hugged me goodbye, she got emotional and, almost instinctively, apologized to the radiation therapist for crying. It struck me—why do we feel the need to apologize for our feelings, especially when they come from love? She reassured her, saying there was nothing to be sorry for. *"This is hard,"* she said. *"And it's okay."*

And with that, it was time. Let's get some tattoos and make a mold.

The mold-making process was fascinating. I laid down on what felt like a half-filled bean bag pillow as they positioned me inside the CT machine. Thankfully, only my chest was inside the scanner—my head was free. If the MRI had been like this, I probably would have been fine.

Once they had the initial images, she adjusted the bean bag, adding air—or maybe sand? I should've asked. Whatever it was, it firmed up but stayed pliable as she molded it around me. After some gentle adjustments, I sat up, then laid back down, trying to reposition myself exactly as before. Without any real instruction, I just knew when it felt "right."

They took a few more images, lined me up with laser beams, and then it was time for the tattoos. Having already come in for clarification, I knew they were just tiny dots, so I wasn't worried. They were completely painless—just small marks, barely noticeable among a few freckles.

During the simulation, I asked the radiation therapist about her job. I asked how long she'd been doing it and if it was as rewarding as it seemed. I told her about my daughter, who works as a chiropractic assistant and absolutely loves patient care. She's a natural nurturer. She shared a little about her schooling and how fulfilling the job was, and suddenly, it hit me—this was exactly the kind of work my daughter would thrive in.

She even wrote down "Radiation Therapist" on a sticky note, along with schools that offer the program in our area. She said if my daughter ever wanted to learn more, she could stop by and talk to her. The kindness in that moment was overwhelming—sometimes, kindness is too small of a word to describe the depth of compassion someone can show.

Afterward, my mom rejoined me, and we sat down with a nurse to go over my treatment plan. She asked about my preferred treatment times since I'd be coming five days a week and walked me through how to care for my skin to prevent radiation burns. When I mentioned that I had already bought My Girls cream after my consultation, she suggested keeping one jar in the fridge for post-treatment cooling and another in the bathroom for after showers. Three applications a day, but never within two hours prior treatment.

My biggest fear had been that the radiation machine would resemble an MRI, and I wasn't sure how I'd handle that. But seeing it in person was a relief—one less thing to worry about.

The concern about radiation burns still lingered, though. So before we left, we stopped by the pharmacy to grab another jar of My Girls cream, just to be extra prepared. I had heard from someone who went through radiation the year before that it was a lifesaver, and with both the nurse and a fellow survivor recommending it, I wasn't taking any chances.

One step closer. One more thing behind me. I could do this.

Chapter 27

# Moments of Clarity
## *Discovering My Inner Strength*

My simulation appointment was scheduled two weeks before my radiation treatments were set to begin. While every appointment carried its own emotional weight, they felt a little lighter now that the cancer had been removed. I no longer had that gnawing fear that it was growing or spreading. My mindset had shifted—I was focused on healing, moving forward, and never looking back. I was sure of one thing: I never wanted to go through this again.

It still felt surreal that this was my life, that I even had to go through radiation at all. My treatment plan consisted of 21 sessions, Monday through Friday. The first 16 would target my full breast and armpit, while the final 5 would be boost treatments, concentrated on the area where the cancer had been. Every Thursday after treatment, I would meet with the radiation oncologist for a quick check-up to monitor my weight, mental health, and skin condition.

I knew it was hard for my mom not to be at every appointment with me, but the financial and logistical strain of traveling so often made it impossible. To keep her connected, I decided I would send her a daily selfie and update her on how each session went. I also promised myself that I would keep a journal throughout treatment—both for my own mental clarity and to track any physical changes.

The weekend before I started radiation, my daughter—who has a real talent for nail art—painted my nails a soft pink and carefully drew a bright pink breast cancer awareness ribbon on one nail of each hand. It was a subtle yet powerful reminder that I wasn't just living through my own diagnosis, but that it was also October—Breast Cancer Awareness Month. I wore my nails proudly, not just for myself but for every woman facing this battle. And in a beautiful show of solidarity, my daughter matched hers to mine.

Day One: Ready or not, it's time.

My husband, my rock, drove me to my first radiation appointment. As we walked into the office, the receptionist greeted me cheerfully, checked me in, and pressed a button to open the doors. She explained that I needed to change into a gown (top only), store my belongings in a locker, and wait in the designated area for someone to bring me back. My husband hugged me, kissed my forehead, and stayed in the waiting room as I stepped through the doors.

I changed into my gown, took a quick selfie for my mom, and locked up my belongings—choosing a locker with a green wristband. Green for luck, right? I walked into the small waiting area and was relieved to see that I was alone. I still felt out of place. My eyes landed on a puzzle sitting on the table, and I immediately sat down to work on it. It was a small comfort, something familiar. It felt symbolic in a way—each piece a part of my journey, slowly coming together.

A radiation therapist appeared in the hallway, smiling warmly. It wasn't the kind of forced cheerfulness that felt out of place, but rather a genuine kindness that put me at ease. She offered me a warm blanket, which I declined—my nerves already had me running hot. As we walked down the hall, she stopped in front of the treatment room and explained that each day, before we entered, I would need to state my name and date of birth. Behind her, I noticed a small area filled with monitors and staff members. It felt oddly official, very clinical, but also reassuring that I was being carefully monitored.

Inside the treatment room, my customized bean bag pillow was already positioned on the table. When I laid down, I could immediately tell if I was in the right position. The therapists adjusted the table up, down, forward, and backward, aligning my tattoo dots with laser beams. Once everything was positioned correctly, they removed my gown from my left breast. I wasn't necessarily uncomfortable, but I was oddly relieved that my right side remained covered. Somehow, being completely exposed would have felt more vulnerable.

Then, it was time. The therapists stepped out of the room. The moment they left, it felt as if all the air had been sucked out. The presence of others had always been a comfort—throughout this entire journey, I had never been alone in a room before. But now, I was. The music playing in the background barely registered. More than anything, I felt the weight of solitude. Radiation was dangerous—that's why everyone else had to leave. It was a sobering thought.

A calm voice came through the speaker: *"Okay, Jessica, let's do a practice breath hold. When you're ready, take a deep breath and hold it."*

I swallowed, my voice a little shaky. *"Okay."*

I took a small, steadying breath, then a deep inhale, holding it for what felt like an eternity. In reality, it was only 30 seconds. Midway through, the voice reassured me: *"You're doing great."* When the timer ran out, she instructed me to exhale and prepare for another breath hold—this time, with the radiation.

Deep breath in. Hold.

*"Almost done... You're doing great."*

We repeated the process three more times.

Finally, the voice returned. *"Great job, we're done for today. You can rest your arms now."*

The radiation therapists reentered the room, lowering the table and guiding me to sit up. They asked how I felt about the session. I admitted that I had been holding my breath like my life depended on it and asked what would happen if I coughed or couldn't hold it long enough. They reassured me that sensors tracked my breathing, and if it became too shallow or unsteady, the radiation would stop automatically.

It was surprisingly quick. From the moment I was called from the waiting area to walking back to the dressing room, the entire process had taken only five minutes. As the therapist walked me down the hall, she reminded me that every session would be exactly the same, and if I ever needed extra time or adjustments, we could always accommodate.

I changed back into my clothes, feeling a sense of relief wash over me. One down. I could do this. I stepped into the waiting room, where my husband was patiently waiting. As I passed by the front desk, the receptionist smiled warmly. *"See you tomorrow, Jessica."*

It was such a small thing—saying my name—but it mattered. It showed that she paid attention, that she cared.

Hand in hand with my husband, I walked to the truck, feeling lighter. The unknown had been the scariest part, but now I knew what to expect. I checked my phone—my daughter had sent me a message: *"You got this! I love you."*

I quickly replied, letting her know it had gone well and that I'd fill her in later. On the drive home, I called my mom. I hoped she could hear the difference in my voice—that I sounded more at ease, more like myself.

I was in the final stretch now.

I felt like I had conquered the day. My mind was at ease knowing what to expect from the process, and I felt so supported—both by my family's presence and their thoughtful messages. When I arrived home, I was greeted with a surprise package from my parents.

As I opened the box, a burst of pink spilled out—everything wrapped in pink flamingo tissue paper and nestled in bright pink paper shreds. The pink, of course, was for breast cancer awareness, but the flamingos? That was just another layer of love. My parents knew how much I adore them.

Growing up in Northern California, one of my favorite places was Apple Hill, especially High Hill Ranch. Every fall, I looked forward to their incredible caramel apples and caramel-covered marshmallows. Now that my parents live on their ranch, it's about a 45-minute drive for them to get there, yet they made the trip just to pick up some of my favorite treats to include in the box.

But that wasn't all. Inside were so many little, thoughtful gifts—a flamingo nail file, pink eye masks, pink cozy socks, pink ice roller, pink gift after pink gift, and most special of all, a custom-made blanket. The blanket was covered in quotes—words of encouragement and positivity that I had posted on my Instagram over the years. Unbeknownst to me, my daughter had done a deep dive, screenshotting them all and secretly sending them to my mom. She never gave the slightest hint that she was planning something so special.

Some of the quotes read:

"Choose kindness and laugh often."

"Let your smile change the world, but don't let the world change your smile."

"Everyone you meet is fighting a battle you know nothing about. Be kind always."

"It's okay to feel all the feels—inside and out."

"My positive attitude starts with gratitude."

"First I drink the coffee, then I do the things."

Each phrase was a reminder of my own strength, my own mindset, reflected back at me. And in the very center of the blanket, a pink heart read: *Wrapped in Love.*

## Chapter 28

# A Moment of Relief
## *Farewell to Radiation, Forever Grateful*

Radiation days all started to blur together—the same routine, day after day. Check-in, change, work on a puzzle, radiation, change again, leave. Within a week, my skin began to feel slightly itchy and tender, but the My Girls cream was doing its job, keeping redness to a minimum.

My husband accompanied me to nearly every appointment, only missing a few when work took him out of town or into a meeting. His commitment to being by my side each day meant the world to me. My friends and family also made sure to check in with me regularly, offering constant support and encouragement.

Going in daily, I became familiar with the radiation team—who was new, who had been there the longest, who had upcoming vacations. On Halloween, my treatment was met with an unexpected dose of whimsy. The receptionist, dressed as Alice from Alice in Wonderland, fit the role perfectly with her blonde hair and sweet demeanor. As I walked toward the dressing rooms, I noticed the entire hallway had transformed into a Wonderland theme, complete with decorated pumpkins in the patient waiting area for a friendly voting contest.

When my radiation therapist came to get me, she was fully committed to her Cheshire Cat costume—tail, ears, face paint, everything. As we made our way down the hall, I saw that the entire team had dressed as characters from Alice in Wonderland—the Queen of Hearts, Tweedledum and Tweedledee, the Mad Hatter, and the White Rabbit. The daily grind of radiation had become predictable, but this was a welcome and heartwarming change.

Later that day, my daughter's close friend stopped by with her baby, who was dressed as an adorable little Tigger. There's something about baby giggles that instantly lifts the spirit, and his sweet smile and infectious laugh were no exception.

Along with bringing him for a visit, she surprised me with a gift—something so thoughtful it brought me to tears. Knowing my love for puzzles, she had found one I'd never seen before—an advent puzzle for Christmas, combining two of my favorite things into one. Each small box represented a day, holding 10 to 15 pieces inside. She encouraged me to complete the first nine before the weekend was over, then continue with two boxes each day after radiation.

Now, I'm no math scholar, but the numbers didn't quite add up. She laughed and assured me that if I followed her plan, the puzzle would be finished on my last day of radiation. I loved the idea, and just like that, it became part of my daily routine—a small but meaningful ritual to mark the journey to the finish line.

It's funny how she got me a Christmas puzzle, because just a few days earlier, something unexpected happened. One afternoon, my daughter and I had gone out for no more than 45 minutes. When we returned, the Christmas tree was up—marking the earliest we had ever put it up in history. I always joke that we celebrate *Hallowgivingsmas* since our tree is always up for Halloween, Thanksgiving, and Christmas. But never before Halloween—well, maybe once or twice, but the tradition was usually to put it up on Halloween day.

Normally, I can't wait to decorate, but this year, Christmas felt different. I was still excited and loved my annual tradition of watching all the new Hallmark Christmas movies, but there was an underlying sadness that dulled the magic I usually felt. I don't think I had even mentioned putting up the tree yet.

But while my daughter and I were out, my husband and our son, moving at warp speed, set it up so that when we walked in, there it was—twinkling and warm, just like my husband's proud smile. It was one of the sweetest surprises, a little piece of holiday magic when I needed it most.

*The Hardest Part:* Radiation's most exhausting aspect wasn't the procedure itself but the fatigue that came with it. I was grateful I wasn't working through treatment because I found myself needing a nap every afternoon. My appointments were mostly at 11 a.m., and by 3 p.m., I'd be asleep.

The My Girls cream became a crucial part of my routine. I had looked up radiation burns—something I desperately wanted to avoid—so I was diligent about applying it. And for the most part, it worked. But despite my best efforts, I missed a spot—the crease of my armpit. By day 15, the area was darker, irritated, and itchy. A few days later, it resembled an old curling iron burn I once saw on my moms friend's forehead—a small patch of burnt skin. Three days after that, the skin cracked. Two more days and it had peeled, exposing raw skin. The pain was intense, but thankfully, my last treatment was just around the corner.

My radiation oncologist prescribed Silvadene cream, instructing me to stop using My Girls until the raw skin healed. A week later, when the pain was unbearable, I messaged my radiation team through MyChart, asking if there was anything else I could do. They had me stop by and handed me a bag containing gloves and RadiaDres Gel Sheets—cooling gel pads that, oddly enough, looked like slices of ham. Since my burn was in my armpit, keeping the pad in place was tricky, but whenever I could sit still for an hour, I'd tuck my "ham slice" in and feel immediate relief.

By day nine of the burn it had quadrupled in size, revealing even more raw skin. It took nearly a month for the area to heal completely.

*A Silver Lining:* Remember when I said my daughter was one of the most caring people I knew? And that the kind radiation therapist had inspired me to mention to my daughter that she'd make a great radiation therapist? Throughout my treatment, we talked about it more, and the radiation team mentioned she could shadow them for a day. She was all in. I passed along her info, and though she chose not to shadow at a time when I was there—it would have been too hard for her—she went and observed for four hours. She loved it. So much so that she looked into school, and now, she's starting in the summer. A reminder that even in the hardest times, good things can still unfold.

My mom had given me a copy of each book in her series, *The Marshal Series* (by Robin Lyons - unapologetic plug for my mama). Inside all four books, she had written a short message—words of encouragement about escaping reality and getting lost in a good story. I wish I had taken a picture of each message to keep, but the sentiment stayed with me.

I brought the books to the waiting room and placed them on the little library shelf and sent my mom a picture. Over time, I noticed a few had disappeared, picked up by someone in need of a distraction. It made me smile—my first small step in giving back and sharing my mom's talent with the world.

*The Final Treatment*: On my last day of radiation, my daughter took off work to be with me and since my husband had a work meeting he couldn't miss it would be just the two of us. I wanted to do something special to thank the radiation team, so a week before my last treatment I reached out to a local bakery and ordered custom treats—a dozen vanilla cupcakes with pink frosting and a dozen heart-shaped sugar cookies, each decorated with a pink breast cancer ribbon and the words *Thank You*. Along with the treats, I wrote a heartfelt card, expressing my gratitude for their kindness and compassion.

During treatment, I had often read the cards lining the hallways from past patients. At first, I thought it was sweet. But a week in, I understood why there were so many. The experience was monumental, the people unforgettable. Their kindness made an otherwise difficult journey bearable.

My youngest son decided to go with my daughter and me to my final appointment, though he chose to stay in the car, offering support from a distance. My daughter and I walked in together, ready for the last treatment.

I hadn't expected my final treatment to be so emotional. As I lay there, I struggled to take a deep breath and hold it as required. The more I struggled, the more I felt overwhelmed. And the more overwhelmed I felt, the more I feared I was holding up the next patient. Fighting back tears, I pushed through. It wasn't perfect, but I got through it.

When getting into position for my treatment we talked about how my daughter had taken the day off to be with me. Unbeknownst to me, one of the radiation therapists had gone to get my daughter from the waiting room and she had been outside the radiation room waiting for my treatment to be over. Not only did they surprise me with bringing her back there, they also surprised me with something unexpected—a small gong for me to ring. My daughter quickly pulled out her phone to capture the moment. I hadn't realized how much this milestone would mean until I stood there, surrounded by the people who had been part of my journey, ready to mark the end of this chapter.

They spoke kind, heartfelt words about my strength and perseverance, and I thanked them sincerely for all they had done to support me through one of the hardest chapters of my life. As I reached for the mallet—with its soft, padded end meant to create a gentler sound than the usual metal-on-metal ring—I could feel the emotions welling up. This moment was bigger than I expected.

With a steady breath, I tapped the gong. The sound echoed softly through the room, carrying the weight of everything I had faced—the pain, the fear, the strength, and the courage. It wasn't just a gong; it was a symbol of survival, of resilience, of every step I had taken to get here.

I had been smiling up until that moment. But as the sound filled the space, it hit me.

I had no idea I'd be ringing a bell. I always thought that was reserved for the women facing the toughest battles—the ones enduring chemo, the ones fighting through the hardest diagnoses.

I made it. Made it through the lumpectomy. Made it through radiation.

I made it through cancer.

## Chapter 29

# Lessons Carried Forward
## *A Moment to Reflect*

This entire journey has felt surreal, and finishing radiation was no different. Every day took its toll—physically and emotionally draining in ways I never expected. Throughout the 21 treatments, I saw a few other patients in passing, yet I felt out of place. No one else seemed to be anywhere close to my age.

One day during radiation, as I walked past the puzzle table on the way to the dressing room, I noticed a woman sitting there—not in a gown, but in regular clothes. It caught my attention because that waiting room was for patients in gowns. After changing into my gown, I sat across from her, and she greeted me with warmth. Without hesitation, she asked if I had breast cancer. It felt strange to be asked so directly, but given that we were in a radiation oncology office, the assumption was fair.

I told her yes—I had breast cancer. She shared that she was in her first week of treatment, while I was in my last. She admitted she was scared and said radiation made her anxious. We talked for a while, and I mentioned the My Girls cream, encouraging her to give it a try. She said she'd pick some up after her appointment. Before we said goodbye, she told me that just talking with me had already made her feel a little better.

In that moment, something clicked: I'm meant to help others through this. I've always wanted to do something meaningful—whether through work or volunteering—and maybe this is it.

For now, I've started by donating puzzles. I found such comfort in working on them at the treatment center each day, and during my time there, I watched four different puzzles get completed. Clearly, I wasn't the only one who found them soothing. I usually do 1,000-piece puzzles, but I noticed the center had 500-piece ones. So now, I buy those instead, and whenever I finish one, I drop it off at the center so someone else can find a little peace in the process—just like I did.

After radiation ended, I had a few weeks to rest and recover before my daughter's childhood best friend came to visit for the first time since we moved from Missouri. I knew we'd be busy every day, showing her the sights and making memories. A few days later, my parents flew up and joined us for Thanksgiving. We had a house full and it made my heart happy to see my daughter laughing and having fun—something she hadn't done in months. She had carried so much worry for me, her thoughts consumed by my diagnosis. Seeing her let go of that, even for a little while, was everything.

It was also a relief for my mom to see that I was okay.

The next steps were simple: a follow-up with my oncologist, then a final visit with my radiation oncologist. Both appointments were scheduled for December, and I felt hopeful that I'd be able to step into 2025 with this chapter behind me—a clean slate. I had the surgery. I completed radiation. Two weeks post-radiation, I started Tamoxifen as instructed. I was doing everything I needed to do to move forward.

When I took a moment to reflect on everything I'd been through, I shared a post on Instagram. The heart of it was simple: this had been the hardest thing I'd ever gone through. And I still stand by that.

There was a Tony Robbins quote that kept echoing in my mind, but I couldn't quite put my finger on the exact wording. I tried Googling it, but still couldn't find it—so I reached out to the one person I knew would know: my brother, who has a mind like a vault when it comes to Tony Robbins quotes. Without missing a beat, he replied, *"Where focus goes, energy flows."*

That was it. That's exactly what I needed to hear.

From that moment on, I made a conscious decision—not to dwell on cancer. I didn't even want to use the word remission. In my post, I wrote: *"I am cancer-free."* Because

I refuse to live in fear, waiting for the other shoe to drop. I don't want to give cancer any more negative energy than it's already taken.

Then, it was time to find peace with my diagnosis. With just two more appointments left, I finally had space to breathe. I don't think true healing begins until treatment ends. Every single day up until then had been filled with cancer—appointments, research, tests, surgeries, treatments, endless conversations. It's all-consuming. There's hardly room to process, let alone accept.

Navigating my diagnosis and treatments around the holidays was tough. Normally, I aim to have my home look like the Christmas section at Hobby Lobby, but this year was different. Maybe it was the exhaustion from radiation, or maybe it was how much space my diagnosis took up in my mind. Whatever the reason, the decorations were fewer, the energy lower—but I appreciated that no one in my family pointed it out.

Still, I made sure to keep some traditions alive. I got us our matching pajama bottoms for our annual family photo. I didn't take as many pictures on Christmas Day or even during our FaceTime celebrations with my parents, brother, and later with my son and his girlfriend, but that was okay. I was just happy to be present, soaking in the moments rather than documenting them.

I did, however, try something new. A friend got me out of the house and took me to her colleague's farm to make wreaths. It was so much fun to step outside my routine and do something creative. Luckily for me, she was a pro at it, so with her guidance, my wreath turned out pretty decent. Beforehand, we wandered through a few antique shops, chatting—not just about cancer, but about life. It was a much-needed break, a reminder that joy could still be found in the small, unexpected moments.

I had joined a Facebook group called *Breast Cancer Support - We Can Do This Together*, and one post stuck with me. A woman shared a quote from Ernest Hemingway: *"In our darkest moments, we don't need solutions or advice. What we yearn for is simply human connection—a quiet presence, a gentle touch. These small gestures are the anchors that hold us steady when life feels like too much."*

There is no magic fix to make this easier. No words to take away the pain. Everyone copes differently—some avoid it, some offer unwavering support—but at the core, almost everyone just wants to make the diagnosis feel a little less lonely.

I often wondered if people looked at me and saw someone who had changed. Because when I looked at myself, I didn't see the old me. I saw someone who was functionally depressed. I'd smile. I'd enjoy moments. I'd find happiness in bits and pieces. But deep down, I felt an undeniable sadness—one that lingered, heavy and constant. I don't know how long it will take for that weight to fully lift.

Like the Butterfly Effect—small shifts that ripple into something greater. I may not know what's ahead, but I do know this: I am still here, still standing, still finding my way.

## Chapter 30

# A Fork in the Road
## *Choosing a Path Forward*

My radiation oncology appointment was postponed until January—so much for wrapping it all up in 2024! But that wasn't the only thing that didn't go as planned.

At my follow-up with my oncologist, a conversation caught me completely off guard. In the whirlwind of appointments, discussions, and stress, I somehow missed that we would be talking about ovarian suppression. Afterward, I went back and checked the clinical notes in MyChart—sure enough, it was mentioned. But at the time, I must have categorized it as a problem for later. I had been in survival mode.

My oncologist laid out the options. The best course of action, he explained, would be to get Lupron shots every three months to induce and maintain menopause, significantly reducing estrogen and progesterone production. Because my body would be going into menopause much earlier than it naturally would, he also recommended Zometa infusions to help strengthen my bones. On top of that, he suggested switching from Tamoxifen to an aromatase inhibitor, Arimidex.

I had no idea that fat cells convert to estrogen through an enzyme called aromatase. Blocking that process, combined with ovarian suppression, would be a double whammy to protect me from recurrence.

But something about it didn't sit right with me.

I sat with the information for a couple of days before sending a message to my oncologist, asking if a full hysterectomy—ovaries and all—could be an alternative. I didn't need them anymore. My youngest is 16. And honestly, the idea of finally getting relief from the monthly premenstrual symptoms that have plagued me for years was an appealing bonus.

He responded that it was a reasonable option and recommended a consultation with a gynecologist, who could go over the pros and cons in more detail. I quickly set up an appointment, grateful I didn't have to wait long.

The doctor was incredibly kind and explained that while my oncologist had initially mentioned five years of Lupron shots, given my age, it would likely be closer to ten years. Ten years of shots! That sounded unbearable. Between the Lupron shots every three months and Zometa infusions every six months, my future suddenly felt like an endless cycle of medical interventions—something I wasn't sure I could live with.

At the same time, it felt strange—almost wrong—to go against the advice of my oncologist, a specialist in cancer treatment. He knew far more about this than I did. The conflict within me was overwhelming. I fought hard to keep my emotions in check, but the tears came anyway.

The doctor was sympathetic, reminding me that this was my decision. No one else could make it for me.

Unfortunately, she no longer performed hysterectomies, which made it even more frustrating that the scheduling department had set me up with her for a surgical consult. But despite that, her reassurance meant the world to me.

My husband had come with me to the appointment, which was comforting. He knows how I feel, and when I struggled to hold back tears, he stepped in and spoke for me. On the way home, we talked about everything. He asked how I felt about my options—even though he already had an idea—careful not to push me in any direction.

I took time to weigh my choices, but deep down, I already knew what felt right.

I was ready to move on. And the thought of getting a shot every three months for ten years, plus IV infusions every six months for three years, just wasn't for me.

I sent a message to the gynecologist, thanking her for her time and understanding, and letting her know I wanted to move forward with the full hysterectomy. I asked how I could get in with someone who could perform the surgery. She responded quickly, letting the scheduling department know, and soon after, I got a call to set up an appointment with a different gynecologist who does perform hysterectomies.

Walking into the second consultation, I felt much more confident. The first appointment had reassured me that I wouldn't be judged for making this choice.

Of course, I wasn't looking forward to another surgery. It felt like I had just had one. Another surgery meant another recovery. And yet, I knew—without hesitation—that this was the right path for me.

More than anything, I wanted to move forward. I knew that frequent shots and infusions would only keep cancer at the forefront of my mind, making it impossible to ever feel like I had moved on.

It's taken me a long time to accept that I will never be able to put this completely behind me. For so long, I believed that once I finished my follow-up appointments with both oncologists, I could close this chapter. But that's not how this works.

I might not be leaving it all behind, but I am moving forward.

One step at a time.

## Chapter 31

# Finding Refuge
## *Mountains, Water, and the Path to Peace*

I've always loved being near water—rivers, lakes, oceans, pools, hot tubs—you name it, I love it. That deep connection to water is one of the biggest reasons we moved to the Pacific Northwest, where endless breathtaking places offer an escape when life feels overwhelming.

I told my husband how much I needed to get out, to be in nature, to hear the sound of running water. There's one place in particular that soothes my soul—Moulton Falls on the East Fork of the Lewis River. Words can't fully capture its beauty. Towering evergreen trees, moss-draped trunks hidden from the sun, crystal-blue water, smooth boulders, and fallen trees polished by rushing currents—it's stunning. The sound of the river brings me peace. During hard times, the atmosphere alone has brought me close to tears. Maybe one day, I'll allow myself to let them fall.

Throughout this entire process, I've taken time to sit with my feelings, and thankfully, my husband is perfectly content with quiet, peaceful drives. We don't need words—we just hold hands, watching the ever-changing landscape around us. As much as I try not to let my thoughts be consumed by my diagnosis, it's impossible to push it away completely. And I think that's okay. It's important to acknowledge every emotion, to honor my own feelings and the feelings of those around me.

Back when my husband was in the military and we were stationed in California, I had two friends I'd meet up with regularly for our Friday coffee dates. But since then, I haven't had that kind of close-knit group of local girlfriends—the ones who gather for dinner, drinks, or just to catch up. The majority of my friends are scattered across the country, but one thing I have come to realize is that I miss having that, and I need to make an effort to get together with the few friends I do have that live nearby.

Jen Delvaux, a woman I follow on Instagram and listen to on her podcast *Not Today Cancer*, once shared something that truly resonated with me—how friendships often change or even fade after a cancer diagnosis, no matter the stage. Curious, I looked into it, and there are many reasons why this happens. But at its core, I believe it comes down to one simple truth: cancer changes the person who is diagnosed. Priorities shift. Time feels more precious. And the way people show up—or don't—becomes more apparent than ever.

I felt this firsthand. A friendship I had cherished for years began to unravel. In hindsight, the shift had been happening gradually, in small, subtle ways that I once brushed off. But my cancer diagnosis brought everything to the surface, accelerating what, deep down, had likely been inevitable.

Back in late September or early October, I came across a local organization called the *Pink Lemonade Project*. I wanted to participate in their annual walk/run, but I was in the middle of radiation and didn't have it in me. 2025, I'm making it happen! It's a women-only event, so my daughter will join me, and I'm sure a few friends will as well.

Pink Lemonade Project also has a mentorship program, and while I've been hesitant to connect with others through shared trauma, I decided to sign up as a mentee. One day, when the clouds clear, I may return as a mentor, but for now, I just wanted to talk to someone who truly understood. Within days, I was matched with a woman who had a similar diagnosis. When she called, we talked for an hour. It was nothing like I expected—no trauma bonding, just a real, refreshing conversation. I don't feel the need to continue with her mentorship, but I see the value in it. I'll support the program in other ways, through donations and participation in their events.

For me, processing this experience happens through reflection and writing. If my story reaches even one person who needs to hear it, then it's all worth it.

I've often said that I'm grateful I never had minimal experience with breast cancer before this. I hope no one else that I know gets this diagnosis, but if someone ever does, I know I'll be able to offer support and empathy in a way I never could have before.

Recently, I came across a term—breast cancer-related imposter syndrome. The more I read about it, the more it resonated with me. Imposter syndrome related to breast cancer is the feeling that your experience with the diagnosis isn't "valid enough" or that you don't truly belong in the cancer community. It can manifest in several ways:

1. Comparing Your Diagnosis to Others – You might feel like your treatment was "easier" than someone else's because you didn't need chemotherapy or a mastectomy, making you question whether you should even call yourself a survivor.

2. Minimizing Your Struggles – You may downplay your pain, fear, or emotional struggles because you think others had it worse, leading to guilt for feeling upset about your own journey.

3. Feeling Like You Don't Deserve Support – You might hesitate to seek support from survivor groups or talk about your experience, fearing that you don't belong because your cancer was caught early, or your treatment wasn't as aggressive as someone else's.

4. Dismissing Your Trauma – You may tell yourself, "It wasn't that bad," or "I should be grateful," even though you've endured a life-changing experience.

5. Struggling to Accept Survivorship – Even after treatment, you might feel like you don't fit the traditional "warrior" or "survivor" narrative, making it hard to embrace healing and moving forward.

Although I can resonate with this deeply, I have to remind myself that every breast cancer journey is valid and mine is no different. No matter the stage, treatment, or outcome. Your feelings and fears are real, and your experience does matter. Healing—both physically and emotionally—looks different for everyone, and you don't need to "prove" your struggle to deserve support and recognition.

## Chapter 32

# A Fragile Heart
## *Carrying the Unspoken Pain*

I know I've said this before, but it's worth repeating—while the lumpectomy and radiation were physically exhausting, the emotional and mental toll has been far more difficult. I don't get much time alone. My husband works a hybrid remote schedule, so he's home often. My daughter works but is usually home in the evenings, unless she's at the gym or with friends. And our youngest son has an unusual hybrid school schedule, meaning he's home a lot too.

I recently came across a quote that said: "She's going to forever say, 'I got this,' even with tears in her eyes, because that's what the strong ones do. It's not that they don't cry for help; they whisper to themselves—one more step, one more fight. No matter how broken they feel, they stand up anyway. That's not weakness; that's a quiet kind of power."

Reading that made me realize something—I am strong. I do have the power to endure and push through. But I often question if I'm truly brave. Bravery, to me, means having a choice. And the truth is, I don't have a choice. I had to face this.

CHAPTER 33

# Choosing Surgery
*Protecting My Future*

I still couldn't believe I was facing another surgery—just six months after my lumpectomy. This time, though, it felt different. Less stressful. This wasn't about treating cancer; it was about preventing it from coming back.

My lumpectomy had been performed at Legacy Health Hospital but my hysterectomy would be done at The Vancouver Clinic as an outpatient procedure. It would be done robotically with the DaVinci machine. One thing I found really helpful was that they required patients to attend a nurse-led class before the surgery.

The class was incredibly informative. Each of us received a packet with direct contact information for the surgical team, a list of medications we'd be prescribed, recovery timelines, and a shopping list of recommended items. The nurse leading the class was part of the surgical team and explained that she or another nurse would be checking in on us every three days after the procedure. She even had a slideshow breaking down the surgery and post-op care. I wasn't too anxious about this surgery, but the class put me even more at ease.

One unexpected downside? The nurse mentioned that getting a tattoo within eight weeks of surgery is discouraged because it taxes the immune system and can affect healing. That was a bummer because I had an appointment scheduled the week after my surgery for my birthday. When I emailed my tattoo artist about it, she responded saying she loved that they mentioned that in the class because it's true—it really does impact healing and how the body reacts to the tattoo.

My surgery was scheduled for February 14, 2025—Happy Valentine's Day. I tried not to let the anxiety build, and it was definitely easier this time around. Knowing that I was eliminating the biggest contributor to my estrogen dominance gave me some peace of mind. Not only did it reduce the risk of breast cancer recurrence, but it also meant potential relief from my premenstrual migraines, backaches, hip pain, sinus pressure, and everything else that came with my cycles. If it didn't? Well, I joked that I'd be checking myself into a loony bin because I would go absolutely bonkers.

My parents flew in for the surgery, and my daughter took the day off work to be there. My husband also took the day off. It's a strange feeling—wanting a support system but also feeling almost too supported. It's an odd balance I still can't quite make sense of.

Telling my youngest son about another surgery was tough. He's struggled to process my diagnosis, not really knowing how to express his emotions or fully understand what's happening. But since this was a preventative surgery and not a reaction to something urgent, I think it was easier for him to accept. I'm convinced sons and daughters process emotional trauma differently.

About a week before surgery, I noticed a tender spot on my left breast. As much as I tried to ignore it, it consumed my thoughts. I told myself I'd get it checked immediately, but no appointments were available. I figured I'd just ask about it during my surgery visit, but with all the moving parts that day, I completely forgot. My husband later admitted he thought about bringing it up but could tell by my demeanor that it wasn't the right time. He was right, it wasn't.

It's hard not to worry. My tumor had been in the outer upper quadrant, and now this tenderness was in the inner lower quadrant—but the same breast. The thought invaded my dreams. One night, I dreamed my mammogram came back positive for breast cancer. Another night, I dreamed my oncologist told me that if I had completed the MRI, we would have caught another tumor. The worst dream was the one where it had progressed too far to treat. I knew I needed to get it checked, if only for my peace of mind. I kept thinking, could my story really be one of breast cancer, surgery, radiation, and then cancer again?

*Surgery Day*

My hysterectomy experience was very different from my

lumpectomy. The Vancouver Clinic ran like a well-oiled machine—efficient, on schedule, and full of kind, attentive surgical nurses.

As I was wheeled down to the operating room, the anxiety crept in. Here I am, six months later, doing this again. In the operating room, they had me move from the bed onto the operating table, explaining the next steps. I told the nurse I was getting anxious, and just as I felt panic creeping in, my gynecologist who was performing the surgery, walked in. She took my hand and reassured me that everything would be okay.

She told me the nurse was about to place an oxygen mask over my face and that I just needed to take a few deep breaths to relax. As she spoke, she rubbed her thumb across the back of my hand in the most natural, comforting way. Then she asked, *"Are you more of a beach or mountain person?"*

I told her I love both, but the ocean fills my soul with happiness.

*"Then just close your eyes,"* she said, *"and imagine the waves, the sound, the sun on your skin. Take a deep breath, and let me take care of you."*

That's the last thing I remember before waking up in recovery, where my mom and husband were waiting.

Unlike my lumpectomy—where I woke up groggy but pain-free—this time I woke up in excruciating pain. Everything hurt. My mom later told me she could see it all over my face before I even spoke a word. The nurse said I needed to eat some crackers before they could administer pain medication through my IV. I had specifically bought gluten-free crackers for this reason, remembering they mentioned it during the nurse-led pre-op class. But in the chaos of that morning, I left them at home. Thankfully, while I was in surgery, my mom and husband ran to the store. Since my mom is also gluten-free, she knew exactly what to get.

I could barely function. I couldn't think, talk, or do anything but sit in pain. My mom broke off tiny pieces of crackers and fed them to me, while my husband gave me sips of my favorite tea—black iced tea with vanilla sweetener from

Starbucks. As soon as the nurse decided I had eaten enough, she gave me the IV pain meds, and thankfully, they kicked in fast.

Once I was more alert, they had me try to walk to the bathroom and empty my bladder before I could be discharged. My husband, my rock through all of this, helped me up and into the bathroom. And if you knew him, you'd know how much this was pushing his boundaries. He's always been grossed out by anything period-related, and here he was, helping me navigate mesh underwear and a pad—a jumbo pad, just like after having a baby.

And in a moment of pure irony, as he was helping me, the pad fell onto the floor. The look on his face was priceless. He had to pick it up.

I laughed—which hurt, but was worth it. Karma at its finest. He even had to go grab another pad for me which I am sure made him cringe the entire time.

Once I was able to walk back to my recovery room and change, I was cleared to go home. I had told myself I wouldn't take pain meds, just like I hadn't with my lumpectomy. But given how I woke up from this surgery, I wasn't so sure I could manage without them.

One thing I appreciated was that my gynecologist had sent my prescriptions to the pharmacy ahead of time, so I already had everything I needed at home. No scrambling. No waiting. Even though I hated the idea of taking pain meds, I also didn't want to feel that level of pain again.

And so, just like that, another surgery was behind me.

CHAPTER 34

# A Lesson in Grace
## *Learning to Heal, Inside and Out*

My mother-in-law made me the perfect heating pad, filled with flaxseeds. It was incredibly soothing to warm it up in the microwave and lay it across my stomach. Our electric reclining couches made a huge difference in keeping me comfortable, though I definitely needed help getting up. Strangely, getting out of bed was easier than getting off the couch—probably because of the height difference and how much core strength was required. Luckily, I had my "support squad" ready to assist, and anytime I needed to get up, someone was quick to jump in and help.

Once the pain meds started wearing off, I became acutely aware of how much effort simple movements required—getting up, sitting down, going to the bathroom, even coughing or sneezing felt more uncomfortable than I had anticipated. Still, the discomfort was manageable. At least for the first day, I knew I would take the pain meds. There was no reason to suffer unnecessarily.

Sleeping was difficult. I usually sleep on my side, but that wasn't an option, so getting comfortable was a challenge. I had ordered a wedge pillow online, and I was so glad I did. It helped keep me slightly elevated in bed, which was far more comfortable than lying flat, and it also made getting up easier.

Recovery from the hysterectomy was strange. When I was in a lot of pain, it was easy to embrace rest and just take it easy. But once I started feeling better, doing nothing became difficult. The recovery guidelines were clear: no lifting over 15 pounds for six weeks, no driving while on pain meds (otherwise, if I could get in and out of the car without wincing, I was probably fine to drive), no sweeping, mopping, vacuuming, or twisting for eight weeks, and no sex or penetration for twelve weeks.

In the early days, I fully embraced "sloth mode" and

Herkel Durkling (a fun Scottish term for lounging around and being lazy). But as soon as I started feeling better, I felt like a burden. I knew I needed to rest, yet I felt embarrassed or guilty for not doing anything. When the floor needed sweeping or the dishes were piled up and knowing I wasn't allowed to handle it was frustrating. The only thing worse than being unable to do it myself was having to ask someone else to do it. It made me feel like I was sitting on a throne, watching my family act as my servants. I knew that wasn't rational, but it's how I felt.

The first time I showered, it took every ounce of energy I had. In fact, I noticed that everything completely drained me. Since my surgery was on a Friday, I didn't get a check-in call from the surgical nurse until Monday. She asked how I was feeling, if I was taking my pain meds, if I was having bowel movements, and whether my incisions looked okay. The next call was on Wednesday, by which time I was feeling much better, but I mentioned how exhausted I was after even the simplest tasks—showering, going up and down the stairs, just moving around. She reminded me that even though the surgery was done robotically and was considered minimally invasive, a full hysterectomy is still major surgery. She explained that my body was using all its energy to heal, and once that healing was complete, it would still take time for my energy levels to be replenished.

The final check-in call came on Friday. I told her that one of my incisions was red and irritated, so she had me send a photo through MyChart. She responded quickly, saying it looked stable and not infected, but that the center incision on the stomach often gets the most irritation since it rubs against clothing. She reminded me—again—that this was a major surgery and that I needed to take my recovery seriously. At a *minimum*, I needed to follow the six-, eight-, and twelve-week restrictions.

Meanwhile, the tender spot on my breast remained on my mind. I had tried to schedule an appointment with my gynecologist, but she was booked until May. Since I was already seeing her for my post-op in two weeks, I decided I would bring it up then. If I forgot, my husband would be there to remind me—one way or another, it needed to be addressed for my peace of mind.

At my post-op appointment, I asked her to check the tender spot. I explained that it had never been tender before, and suddenly, it was, which didn't make sense to me. I knew surgery and radiation had changed my breast tissue and caused some scar tissue buildup, but there shouldn't be pain. Mild as it was, it was still noticeable. She did a quick exam and said she didn't feel anything concerning, but given my history, a mammogram would be the best precautionary step.

On one hand, I had hoped she would just say, "There's no way anything could be there given the radiation and the timeline." But that's not what happened. Instead, she said it was "very unlikely." And while "unlikely" is reassuring, it's still not the same as "impossible."

The Breast Care Center called to schedule a mammogram and ultrasound for the following week. I couldn't shake the feeling of déjà vu. Ideally, the mammogram would show nothing, and the ultrasound wouldn't even be necessary. But I knew they would probably see the hematoma that was still lingering six months later.

I hadn't told many people about this upcoming mammogram—just my husband, my daughter, my parents, and two friends. It's not that I'm embarrassed or afraid. I just don't want anyone worrying about me or treating me like I'm fragile.

All I can do was keep telling myself: *Hopefully, it's nothing.*

# Chapter 35

# The Voice Within
## *Trusting My Gut*

It was time for another follow-up with my oncologist to discuss the next steps. One thing I knew for sure—I no longer had to worry about the Lupron shots to suppress estrogen since my recent hysterectomy and bilateral salpingo-oophorectomy (ovary removal) had already taken care of that. But we still needed to talk about what medication I'd be switching to in place of Tamoxifen and the IV infusions of Zometa.

I was open to starting an aromatase inhibitor, but I wasn't thrilled about the idea of Zometa infusions. From what I had researched, the side effects sounded tough, and I just didn't feel ready to take that on. Maybe one day, but not now. I had a bone density scan scheduled in a few weeks, and depending on the results, my stance might change. If my bone health turned out to be poor, I'd do what was necessary to strengthen them. That's always been a concern of mine—after all, I spent nearly two decades on prednisone due to chronic, unexplained hives, and one of its side effects is weakened bones.

As I've mentioned before, it feels unnatural to go against a doctor's recommendation, but at the end of the day, I have to do what feels right for me. He was very understanding when I told him I wasn't comfortable with the Zometa infusions, at least for now. He assured me he wouldn't push me and that if I ever changed my mind, all I had to do was reach out. That acceptance meant a lot. I had worried that he might, even unintentionally, make me feel guilty—like I wasn't taking my diagnosis seriously enough. But I know I've taken it seriously. I've done everything I can to ensure I never have to go through this again.

If my bone density test comes back normal, the plan is to continue monitoring every two years. The hysterectomy combined with taking an aromatase inhibitor puts me at a higher risk for osteoporosis—a double whammy. Through all of this, I've learned so much about estrogen, like how it actually helps maintain bone strength, how fat cells convert into estrogen, and it helps protect the heart by keeping cardiovascular tissue healthy and preventing inflammation that contributes to plaque buildup in arteries. Estrogen also plays a role in cognitive functions, including learning, memory, and mood, and may help protect the brain from damage and cognitive decline. It's incredible how little I knew about my own body before this, but I doubt I'm alone in that.

I once read that one of the hardest things about a cancer diagnosis is realizing that even after the surgeries and treatments, it's never really over. That couldn't be more accurate. I had hoped to put all of this behind me, but I've had to accept that it will always be a part of me. Now, my focus has to shift to figuring out how to live as this new version of myself. I feel stuck in limbo—changed but unsure of how to fully move forward.

Recently my daughter played Dolly Parton's 9 to 5, a song that would normally have me belting out the lyrics. But I didn't. And she noticed. She told me I don't have the same energy I used to, and as much as it stung to hear, she was right. That has to change. I don't want to lose the silly, carefree parts of myself because of this.

## Chapter 36

## Bones Tell a Story
### *Establishing a Baseline*

I wasn't nervous at all about the bone density scan, the DEXA, mostly because my mom had one and had explained it to me. For extra reassurance, I Googled it. At first, I was worried it would be done via MRI, which seemed literally impossible for me, but my fears were quickly put to rest when I learned how simple the procedure actually was.

The morning of my scan, I made sure to wear a t-shirt, knowing that once I got to the imaging department, my nerves might kick in. The last thing I wanted was a hot flash on top of anxiety-induced heat. Walking into that space, I felt the weight of past trauma—I still curse that damn MRI tube. My heart rate was definitely a little higher than normal, even though I logically knew I wasn't there for an MRI or anything remotely similar. But my body didn't care about logic; it remembered.

As the technician walked me back to the DEXA room, I mentioned my three failed MRI attempts. She reassured me that the DEXA scan was nothing like that.

The room itself was surprisingly calming, with dim overhead lighting instead of the usual harsh fluorescents. The exam table was basic, and the scanner sat alongside it, almost like a desk lamp that would move up and down depending on the area being scanned. She explained that she would scan my shins, hips, and lower back. For the hip and lower back scans, she placed a large cushion under my legs, positioning them at a 90-degree angle so my back and hips could lay flat. Unlike other imaging tests I'd had, she didn't leave the room during the scan, which reassured me that this was a simple, low-stress procedure.

The whole thing took all of five minutes, and I was on my way. She explained that once the radiologist reviewed the images and made their notes, they would be sent to my doctor, who would follow up with me about the results.

Another item checked off the list. Going forward, I'll have a bone density scan every two years to monitor my bone health and catch any signs of osteoporosis before they progress too quickly.

CHAPTER 37

# Burning Through the Night
## *Sleep, Sweat, Repeat*

For as long as I can remember, I used to say I couldn't wait for menopause. My periods were brutal, and the relentless premenstrual pains drained me month after month. Just as every woman gets a period, every woman will experience menopause at some point. My gynecologist told me the average age for menopause is early 50's, but you're not technically in menopause until you've gone 12 consecutive months without a period. Does that still apply to someone who's had a full hysterectomy? Nope, having your ovaries removed causes an abrupt drop in estrogen and progesterone levels, while natural menopause happens gradually over years as ovary function declines.

I have a friend who had a full hysterectomy about ten years ago. When she visited for the weekend, she brought a fan with her. At the time, I thought it was funny—who travels with a fan? The answer: someone who has hot flashes. My daughter had bought a portable fan for one of her coworkers and said it worked great, so I got myself one. It is a game changer, I can't imagine not having it.

My hot flashes actually started when I was on Tamoxifen, but they weren't as intense as I had imagined. Instead of instant, drenching sweat, it felt more like a heat wave creeping up through my body. Almost like watching a thermometer rise, I could feel the warmth spreading until I was practically boiling. The whole thing lasted less than two minutes, then just as quickly as it came on, it was gone.

After my hysterectomy, I was told I'd be thrown into menopause overnight. Since I was already dealing with hot flashes, I figured it wouldn't get much worse. To my surprise, they actually disappeared for a few weeks. My body ran warmer overall, but the sudden waves of heat were gone. That didn't last. I'm not sure if it was switching to an aromatase inhibitor, the surgery, or both, but soon enough, the hot flashes were back—stronger and more frequent, especially at night.

I don't know why they're worse at night, but they make sleeping nearly impossible. My poor husband bundles up like he's camping in the Arctic while I have the ceiling fan on high, plus a separate fan on my nightstand. My nighttime routine is a constant cycle: covers off, covers on, just the sheet, back to the covers, one leg out, one leg in, all of them off again—on repeat, all night long.

The hardest part about menopause with ER+/PR+ breast cancer is that hormone therapy isn't an option for me. People often suggest I talk to my doctor about hormone therapy, but that's a dead-end road. There are non-hormonal treatments available, but most involve more medications—and more side effects. For now, I'm holding off. But eventually, I'll need to figure something out because quality sleep is not overrated.

Other than hot-flashing my way through life, I'm not entirely sure what else to expect from menopause. It's hard to tell what symptoms are from the surgery, the medication, or menopause itself. Maybe once my body fully heals and adjusts to the new meds, things will start making more sense.

## Chapter 38

# Fear to Freedom
### *The Relief of Knowing*

The morning of my mammogram, I woke up feeling those all-too-familiar premenstrual pains. I thought those days were behind me after my ovaries were removed, yet here I was. It's the strangest sensation and hard to explain—almost like my body was running on autopilot, unaware of the changes. The discomfort always starts the same way: a kink in my neck, like I slept wrong, then a creeping headache, followed by pressure behind my eye and in my sinuses. Soon, the pain spreads—hips aching, back throbbing, and before I know it, I'm battling an unbearable full-body ache. But no matter how I felt, I had to push through. I needed to get this mammogram done.

This one was different from the ones before. The technician placed small stickers with metal beads as markers—one over the area where I felt pain and another, a strip that looked like Frankenstein's scar, across my lumpectomy and lymph node removal scars. She explained that the markers would help distinguish incision sites from abnormalities and ensure the painful area was visible in every image. I had braced myself for extra discomfort since the spot was already tender, but surprisingly, it wasn't much worse than previous mammograms. I mentioned that I still had a hematoma from the lumpectomy, and she made a note of it.

After taking all the necessary images, she had me wait while the radiologist reviewed them. If everything looked fine, I'd be free to go. I hoped for that outcome—I didn't want any déjà vu today.

A few minutes later, she returned and told me she was walking me down to the ultrasound room. My anxiety spiked. I made sure to keep my phone within reach this time, just in case I had to sit alone for a while like last time. I remembered wishing I had something to distract my thoughts.

Once in the ultrasound room, I set my things down beside

me, ensuring my phone was within arm's reach. The technician asked me to raise my left arm above my head and describe the pain—where it was, how long I had felt it, and what it felt like.

I explained that the pain was on the underside of my breast, not constant but sharp if I bumped it or laid on it. She let me know she would have to apply pressure during the scan. I braced myself. It wasn't pleasant, but I needed answers. I needed to know if I was about to go through all of this again.

As she moved the ultrasound wand, I made a passing comment about how difficult it must be to learn how to interpret the images. Unlike any other technician I'd encountered, she actually explained it. She showed me the layers of skin on the screen, pointed out areas of fluid buildup, and identified scar tissue from radiation. She reassured me that, from what she saw, nothing looked alarming—but of course, the radiologist would make the final call.

Once she stepped out, I grabbed my phone to update my mom, husband, and daughter, letting them know I had to go through with the ultrasound. I sent my daughter a quick picture, and she immediately texted back, *"It's going to be okay."* Before I could send the message to my mom and husband, the radiologist walked in.

She had a warm, genuine smile—something I desperately needed in that moment. Then, she said the words I had been holding my breath for:

*"I do not see any masses or anything to be concerned about."*

Relief.

She explained that both the ultrasound and mammogram clearly showed my body was still healing from surgery and radiation. She suggested I start doing lymphatic massages to help move along some of the built-up fluid—something I had been told before but had been slacking on. I made a mental note: No more excuses.

On my way to the car, I texted my daughter the good news. She responded, *"Good, now we have peace of mind. You did good, Mommy."* Once in my car, I sent my mom a voice message and called my husband, but it went to voicemail. Assuming he was on a business call, I simply texted him that everything was okay. Had the news been different, I would have called again—he would have known.

The silence on the drive home felt welcome. My body still ached, and I was exhausted. I needed to lie down. I needed water and crackers—something to settle my stomach, which had turned nauseous.

Once home, I sent quick messages to my aunt and friend to share the good news. Then, I crashed. My body was completely drained, the pain intensifying instead of fading. I curled up on the couch, desperate for relief.

That night, I managed to eat a small bowl of Cheerios—just enough to put something in my stomach before taking a Tylenol PM. Sleep was the only thing my body and mind needed now.

CHAPTER 39

# Silent Battles
## *Bravery, Love, and Letting Go*

Being stuck in a cycle of suffering is exhausting. Mentally, physically, emotionally—it feels like one relentless moment after another, a journey defined by hardship. The toll it takes is undeniable. My stress levels had never been higher, a constant hum vibrating inside me, always present, never fading. Between the diagnosis, surgery, recovery, radiation, more recovery, premenstrual pains, another surgery, another round of healing—most days were filled with discomfort and an underlying sadness. I kept wondering, Where do I go from here? How do I break free from this endless loop and find my way back to the happy, lighthearted person I used to be?

When you're feeling low, it's easy to spiral into everything that's been taken from you. Even as someone who naturally leans toward optimism, I wasn't immune to the why me moments. I threw myself more than a few pity parties. The weight of my diagnosis—the heaviness of watching life go on around me while I felt stuck—hit hard.

But at some point, I knew I had to reclaim myself.

Despite everything, I still believe things happen for a reason. This journey took a lot from me, including a friendship I once thought was going to be a lifelong friendship. Losing that hurt deeply. But I've learned that if someone can't stand beside me in the darkest moments, they don't get to celebrate with me in the light. Cancer brings a harsh but honest clarity.

And as much as I hate that this happened, if it had to be someone—I'm glad it was me and not someone I love. Because I *can* handle it. I am getting through it. And I will take everything I've been through and use it to light the way for someone else still finding their footing in the dark.

My top priority now is getting healthy. Not just to prevent breast cancer from coming back, but to protect myself from everything else this journey has put on my radar—

osteoporosis, cardiovascular disease, insulin resistance, high blood pressure, depression. The loss of estrogen has increased my risk for all of them. My whole life, my weight has been my biggest challenge, but now, for the first time, my mental health feels just as fragile.

But I know myself. And I know that I will not let cancer take everything from me.

More than ever, I am driven. Driven to heal. Driven to rebuild. Driven to live—not just for myself, but for my family, for my future.

## Chapter 40

# Standing Still
## *When Life Pauses but the World Moves On*

Now that I've checked all the boxes—lumpectomy, radiation, hysterectomy—I find myself in limboland. Looking back, I had 28 appointments, 3 failed MRI's, 2 surgeries, 21 radiation treatments, an endless stream of medical visits. Now, the only thing left is a check-in with my oncologist every three months via video call. The sudden shift from constant appointments to almost nothing feels strange.

It's not a bad thing. In fact, I'm grateful. Less medical visits mean I'm making my way through and coming out the other side. But still, the transition feels odd.

I recently listened to a podcast by Mel Robbins where she talked about doing an annual *"life audit."* She scrolls through every photo she took over the past year, from January 1 to December 31, rediscovering memories she may have forgotten or not fully appreciated in the moment. I decided to do the same, and while there were plenty of heavy, heartbreaking photos, there were also so many bright spots—uplifting moments, encouraging quotes, screenshots of breast cancer statistics that gave me hope, family photos, beautiful glimpses of nature. There was so much good that had been overshadowed by my diagnosis.

I see the sadness in my own eyes, and it breaks my heart. That's never been who I am. I've always been a happy person. But even in those difficult times, when I really take a closer look, I can see the moments of joy that were woven throughout—small victories, love, and support that I might have overlooked in the thick of it all.

One thing that isn't talked about enough during a cancer journey is how your life feels like it comes to a screeching halt while everyone else's moves forward. But this doesn't just apply to cancer. I remember when my dad passed away—my world shattered, yet my friends' lives carried on, untouched.

It's not that people don't care; it's just the nature of life. Even within my own household, while my diagnosis affected everyone, their daily routines continued. Life doesn't pause for grief, fear, or uncertainty. I don't think there's a way to change that, but recognizing it helps. It's normal. And eventually, I'll catch up to the world again.

## Chapter 41

# A New Reflection
## *When the Mirror Shows Someone Stronger*

As this book comes to an end, even though my journey continues, I find myself reflecting on all of my emotions, journal entries, writings, and my radiation diary. Even now, reading back through my own words can bring me to tears. I don't think I ever truly gave myself enough credit for how hard this was—or for how strong I had to be to get through it.

At one point, I felt guilty for how much I had changed. But looking back, I realize that not changing would have been impossible. This diagnosis was monumental for me. When I first heard the words *"breast cancer,"* I thought because it was caught early and was highly treatable, that this would be something I'd quickly move past. I assumed it would be mostly painless, just a temporary detour. But it became so much more than that. It altered me, reshaped me. And knowing myself—knowing how deeply I feel things—there was never a world in which this wouldn't have left an imprint on my life.

I hope my story helps you or someone you know—maybe by giving insight into what a Stage 1 grade 2 ER/PR-positive DCIS Invasive Carcinoma diagnosis can look like, or maybe by validating someone else's emotions, no matter their stage. Every feeling—rational or irrational, happy or devastating—is valid. I hope this book brings comfort to you navigating a diagnosis, or perhaps to a family member trying to understand what their loved one is going through.

Yes, I was diagnosed with breast cancer, and yes, it was painful and exhausting. But I was also fortunate—it was highly treatable. Radiation was difficult, but through it, I met incredible people. And perhaps the most unexpected gift of all? It inspired my daughter to pursue radiation oncology so she could help others. That alone made every struggle feel like it had meaning.

Through this, I saw my husband live out our wedding vows—through sickness and health. I know this journey wasn't easy for him either. Watching me struggle, knowing he couldn't take the pain away, was extremely hard on him.

My son in Missouri checked in on me constantly, sending loving texts and FaceTime calls—his way of showing love from afar. My daughter dedicated so much of her time and energy to caring for me in ways I never expected. My youngest son, with his gentle soul, made sure I stayed hydrated during radiation, offering me water every time he walked past. And more than once, he was simply there—wrapping me in a silent hug as I cried, never trying to fix it, just holding space for me when I needed it.

My mom sent me the most thoughtful, funny, and encouraging cards—little bursts of love in my mailbox. But more than that, she flew from Sacramento to Portland multiple times just to be with me. My dad, always busy with ranch life, made the time to fly up too—helping in his own way, tackling a few of my husband's "honey-do" list, and making countless trips to and from the airport, a small but meaningful act of love.

My in-laws sent many texts, cards, and care packages. My aunt sent beautiful flowers and heartfelt messages, constantly reminding me how much she loves me. My brother helped me see the bigger picture—reassuring me that breast cancer wasn't going to define me or defeat me. He grounded me when my emotions threatened to overshadow logic, bringing clarity when I needed it most. Friends checked in regularly, offering words of encouragement, thoughtful advice, and helpful healing tips, each message a small but powerful reminder that I wasn't facing this journey alone.

I've also come to understand that not everyone walks this path the same way. My mother-in-law went through breast cancer many years ago, but she chose to keep her experience private. I'll never fully understand that decision, and I think about her often—especially now that I know firsthand just how difficult this journey can be. The thought of her carrying that weight quietly, even with my father-in-law by her side, fills me with sadness. I can't imagine facing this without a circle of support. If I could go back, I wouldn't have asked how I could help—I would have just shown up. I would have made them dinner and left it at the door. I would have said, *"I'm taking you to treatment today,"* because now I know how deeply those small, simple gestures matter when your body is tired and your heart is heavy.

If you know someone going through challenging times, don't wait for them to ask for help. Just do it. Most of us don't want to burden others, but when help is offered, when someone steps in and lightens the load—it makes a difference. It's easy to get wrapped up in the busyness of our own lives and forget to check in, and assume everyone is okay. I've been guilty of it too. But with all the tools we have—phones, calendars, reminders—we can choose to be intentional. Make the call. Send the text. Reach out. Because sometimes, like me, you don't realize what someone is going through until life brings it painfully close to home. Not all struggles are visible. Not all struggles are shared. A simple message, a handwritten card, a small act of kindness can mean more than you'll ever know.

Making the effort to connect isn't just for them—it's for you too. Showing up for the people you love, especially when they need it most, is one of the most meaningful things we can do. And if you've let these simple gestures fall to the wayside, don't be hard on yourself. We don't always know what's going on with other people, and we all falter—you don't know what you don't know.

Here's what I do know:
*I am a warrior.*
*I made it through.*
*I will be okay.*

If I could leave you with one final thought, it would be this: Sometimes, bad things happen to good people. Hard times don't wait for an invitation. And in those moments, when you feel like you can't push through—when you feel emotionally drained, physically exhausted, or just broken—you are so much stronger than you think. And even in the hardest times, there are still good things to be found.

# The Technical Stuff
## *Resources and Diagnosis Breakdown*

It can be incredibly overwhelming trying to understand the flood of information that comes with a diagnosis—mammogram results, pathology reports, medical terminology—it's a lot to take in. That's why I felt this topic deserved its own section. I want to provide helpful context and resources for anyone feeling as confused and lost as I was. Hearing the information is one thing, but truly understanding it is something else entirely. I remember feeling silly asking my oncologist to simplify things so I could actually grasp what was happening. But the truth is, I wasn't in a place to understand at that time—I was just trying to survive the onslaught of information, the emotions and the diagnosis.

Since then, I've had the space to go back and make sense of it all, and I hope what I've learned can help you too. Even if your diagnosis isn't the same as mine, the explanations and resources I share here might help you better understand your own. That said, I want to be absolutely clear: I'm not a doctor, and I'm not qualified to interpret anyone else's reports. I'm simply sharing what I learned to help paint a clearer picture—for myself.

I remember feeling especially confused when I kept seeing women online say they had DCIS *or* Invasive Carcinoma, and yet my pathology report read: *"Present in association with invasive carcinoma and DCIS."*

I panicked, thinking I had two types of cancer in two different areas. But after many, many hours of Googling and reading, I came to understand that it's actually common to have both. The cancer often starts as DCIS, and in some cases, a portion of it becomes invasive. They can coexist—like a cluster of DCIS with a small area that has started to invade nearby tissue.

Here's what my diagnosis looked like: Stage 1 Grade 2 ER/PR Positive DCIS + Invasive Carcinoma HER2-

Let's break that down:

Stage 1: This means the invasive part of the cancer is small (under 2 cm) and hasn't spread to lymph nodes or other parts of the body. It's considered early-stage and highly treatable.

Grade 2: Means the cancer falls somewhere in the middle—not the most aggressive, but not the least either. It's considered a moderate-risk category. Under the microscope, the cells appear somewhat abnormal and tend to grow at a moderate rate. It's important to note the difference between grade and stage: grade refers to how abnormal the cancer cells look and how quickly they're likely to grow, based on the pathologist's evaluation. Stage, on the other hand, describes how far the cancer has spread throughout the body.

ER/PR Positive: The cancer cells have estrogen (ER) and progesterone (PR) receptors. In other words, they use these hormones to grow. This is actually a good thing—it means the cancer is more likely to respond well to hormone-blocking treatments like tamoxifen or aromatase inhibitors, which help reduce the risk of recurrence.

DCIS + Invasive Carcinoma: DCIS (ductal carcinoma in situ) is considered the earliest form of breast cancer—it means the abnormal cells are still contained within the milk ducts and haven't yet spread into surrounding tissue. Invasive carcinoma means that some of the cancer cells have broken through the duct wall and started invading nearby breast tissue. It's common for both to be found together, especially if the cancer began as DCIS and progressed.

HER2 Negative (HER2-): HER2 stands for Human Epidermal Growth Factor Receptor 2, a protein that helps cancer cells grow and divide. HER2 negative means my cancer doesn't have too much of this protein, so it doesn't grow as aggressively as HER2 positive cancers.

# Resources I found helpful:

**American Cancer Society: Understanding Your Pathology Report: Breast Cancer -** *https://www.cancer.org/cancer/diagnosis-staging/tests/biopsy-and-cytology-tests/understanding-your-pathology-report/breast-pathology/breast-cancer-pathology.html*

**Breastcancer.org: Understanding Your Pathology Report** - *https://www.breastcancer.org/pathology-report*

**Breast Cancer Now:** *https://breastcancernow.org/*

**Pink Lemonade Project:** *https://pinklemonadeproject.org/virtually-pink/*

**Jen Delvaux:** *https://www.jendelvaux.com/*

**Jen Delvaux and her husband do a podcast called - Not Today Cancer podcast:** *https://podcasts.apple.com/us/podcast/not-today-cancer/id1436449587*

**The Breast Cancer Podcast: This podcast is great because the host is a breast surgeon and she has conversations with some amazing other specialists, one I found particularly helpful was called Do you understand your breast pathology? If you want to look back for that one it was on 12/10/2024 -** *https://podcasts.apple.com/us/podcast/the-breast-cancer-podcast/id1565403179*

Every cancer diagnosis is unique—just as every treatment plan is carefully tailored by an oncologist to fit the individual needs of each patient. My hope is that the resources I've shared here will offer some clarity during what is often an incredibly confusing and overwhelming time.

Looking back, I've realized how important it is to educate yourself as much as possible. If something doesn't make sense, write it down. Bring your questions with you to your appointments—because once you're sitting in that room, it's easy to forget what you meant to ask. There's so much information being thrown at you, and it's completely normal to feel scattered or overwhelmed. Having a written list can help keep you grounded and ensure your voice is heard.

You don't have to be fearless—just brave enough to take the next step.

Connect with me on Instagram @**RootedInPink**, where I share my journey, reflections, and insights in hopes of supporting and connecting with others.

# About the author

My name is Jessica Dickens — mom to three amazing kids and wife to my high school sweetheart. In 2022, I had my first clear mammogram at 42. I skipped one year. In 2024, my world changed when I was diagnosed with Stage 1 Grade 2 ER/PR+ breast cancer. I've always been an optimist, so I was thrown off by the onslaught of fear, anger, and grief that came with my diagnosis. Journaling became a way for me to process those emotions and make sense of a life that suddenly felt uncertain.

I'm lucky to have the most amazing and supportive family, who stood by me through every high and low. You'll read that throughout the book. What started as a personal outlet soon became a deeper mission: to share my story so that no one walking this road would ever feel alone, like I did, even though I had my supportive family.

This book isn't polished for perfection — it's honest, unfiltered, and full of both the beautiful and the brutal moments that come with a breast cancer diagnosis. It's my hope that by keeping it real and raw, my words will meet you exactly where you are, and remind you that even when life sucks, it will get better.

*xoxo,*
*Jessica*

www.ingramcontent.com/pod-product-compliance
Lightning Source LLC
Chambersburg PA
CBHW020203090426
42734CB00008B/920